Beginning React and Firebase

Create Four Beginner-Friendly Projects Using React and Firebase

Nabendu Biswas

Apress®

Beginning React and Firebase: Create Four Beginner-Friendly Projects Using React and Firebase

Nabendu Biswas
Bhopal, India

ISBN-13 (pbk): 978-1-4842-7811-6   ISBN-13 (electronic): 978-1-4842-7812-3
https://doi.org/10.1007/978-1-4842-7812-3

Managing Director, Apress Media LLC: Welmoed Spahr
Acquisitions Editor: Louise Corrigan
Development Editor: James Markham
Coordinating Editor: Jessica Vakili
Copyeditor: Kim Wimpsett

Distributed to the book trade worldwide by Springer Science+Business Media New York, 1 NY Plaza, New York, NY 10014. Phone 1-800-SPRINGER, fax (201) 348-4505, e-mail orders-ny@springer-sbm.com, or visit www.springeronline.com. Apress Media, LLC is a California LLC and the sole member (owner) is Springer Science + Business Media Finance Inc (SSBM Finance Inc). SSBM Finance Inc is a **Delaware** corporation.

For information on translations, please e-mail booktranslations@springernature.com; for reprint, paperback, or audio rights, please e-mail bookpermissions@springernature.com.

Apress titles may be purchased in bulk for academic, corporate, or promotional use. eBook versions and licenses are also available for most titles. For more information, reference our Print and eBook Bulk Sales web page at http://www.apress.com/bulk-sales.

Any source code or other supplementary material referenced by the author in this book is available to readers on GitHub via the book's product page, located at www.apress.com/978-1-4842-7811-6. For more detailed information, please visit http://www.apress.com/source-code.

Printed on acid-free paper

Table of Contents

About the Author

Nabendu Biswas is a full-stack JavaScript developer who has been working in the IT industry for the past 16 years and has worked for some of the world's top development firms and investment banks. He is a popular tech blogger who publishes on `dev.to`, `medium.com`, and `thewebdev.tech`. He is an all-round nerd, passionate about everything JavaScript, React, and Gatsby. You can find him on Twitter @nabendu82.

About the Technical Reviewer

Alexander Nnakwue is a self-taught software engineer with experience in back-end and full-stack engineering. Nnakwue loves to solve problems at scale. He is currently interested in startups, open source web development, and distributed systems. In his spare time, he loves watching soccer and listening to all genres of music.

CHAPTER 1

Setting Up and Deploying a ReactJS Project with Firebase

In this chapter, you will learn about Firebase, which is a set of tools provided by Google. You will also learn how to deploy a simple React app through Firebase hosting.

Introduction to Firebase

Firebase is not just a database but a set of tools; it is often called a *back-end-as-a-service* (BaaS). Firebase contains a variety of services, as listed here:

- *Authentication*: User login and identity
- *Real-time database*: Real-time, cloud-hosted, NoSQL database
- *Cloud Firestore*: Real-time, cloud-hosted, NoSQL database
- *Cloud storage*: Massively scalable file storage
- *Cloud functions*: Serverless, event-driven back-end functions
- *Firebase hosting*: Global web hosting
- *ML Kit*: An SDK for common machine learning tasks

Firebase makes it easy for front-end developers to integrate a back end into their application, without creating any API routes and other back-end code. Figure 1-1 shows an example of a traditional web app, which does API requests to the server from the

© Nabendu Biswas 2022
N. Biswas, *Beginning React and Firebase*, https://doi.org/10.1007/978-1-4842-7812-3_1

client apps. The rest of the code is handled by the server. As you can see in Figure 1-1, Firebase eliminates the back-end work, and you communicate directly with Firebase, hosted on the Google platform with an SDK.

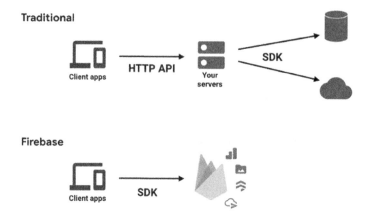

Figure 1-1. *Firebase*

It's extremely easy to build a project in the Firebase back end with ReactJS as the front end. If you made the same project in MERN (meaning MongoDB, Express, ReactJS, NodeJS), it would take more time and would be far more complicated as you would need to make the back-end APIs in NodeJS.

The other thing I find easy to do in Firebase is the authentication part. Authentication used to be one of the most complicated parts of JWT authentication, but with Firebase you need only a few lines of code. Even better, you get all types of authentication.

Firebase hosting is also extremely easy to use for your ReactJS apps, and that is what we are going to look at in this book.

Creating a Firebase Account

To work with Firebase, you just need a Google account. So, go to Firebase site at `https://firebase.google.com/` and click **Go to console** in the top-right corner. You need to be logged in with your Google account to do so, as shown in Figure 1-2.

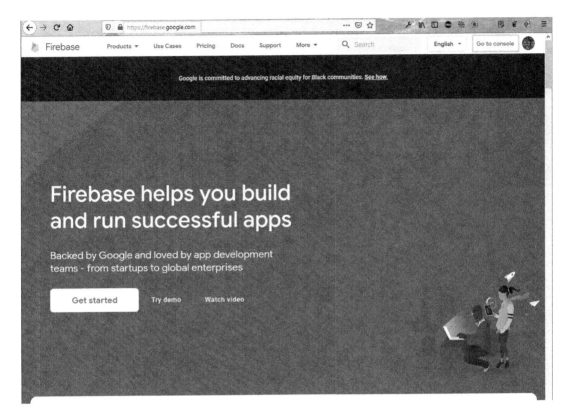

Figure 1-2. *Firebase site*

Setting Up Hosting

Click the **Add project** link on the page, as shown in Figure 1-3. Since I have a lot of projects, the figure shows them on this page. For your first time, you will see only the **Add project** link.

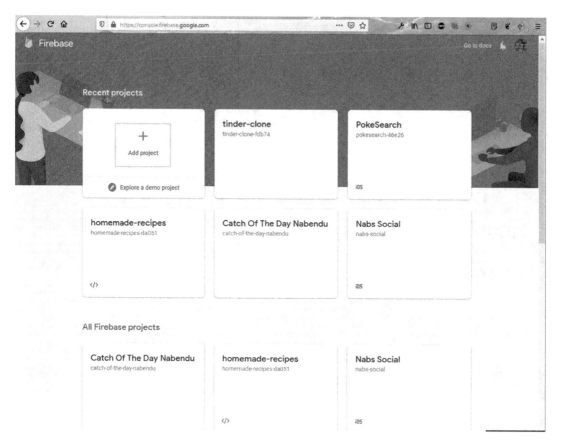

Figure 1-3. *Adding a project*

On the page that opens, give the project a name like **final-space-react** and click the **Continue** button, as shown in Figure 1-4.

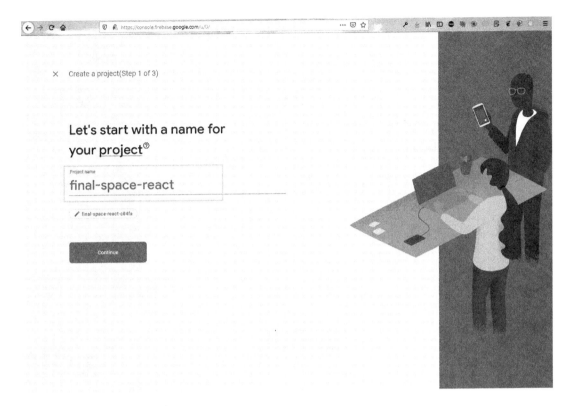

Figure 1-4. *Naming the project*

On the next page, click the **Create project** button after disabling Google Analytics, as shown in Figure 1-5. We are disabling Google Analytics as we're creating a demo project here. If you intend to deploy your app in production, you should keep it enabled.

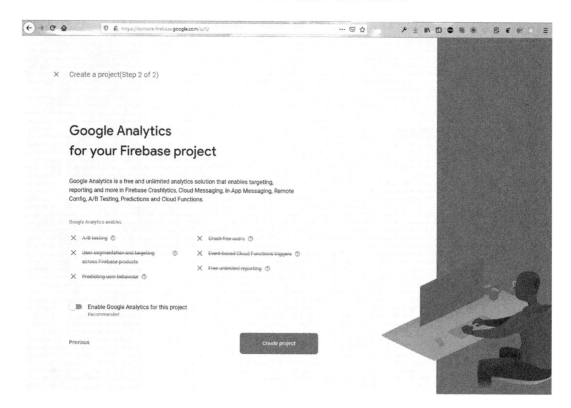

Figure 1-5. *Creating a project*

After some time, you will see the screen shown in Figure 1-6. Here, you need to click the **Continue** button.

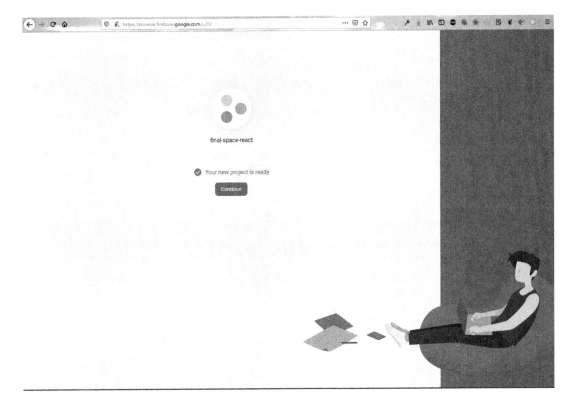

Figure 1-6. *Continuing*

Now, click the **Settings** icon at the top-left corner of the screen, as shown in Figure 1-7. After that, click **Project settings**.

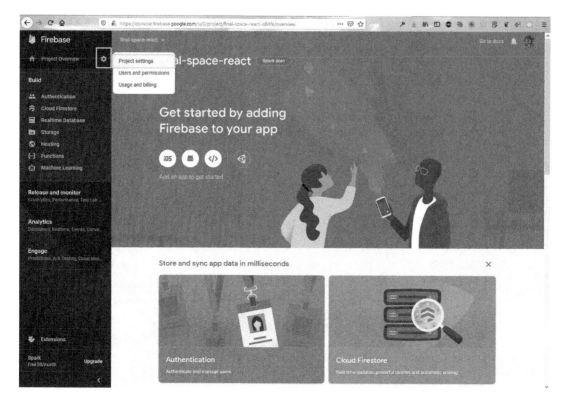

Figure 1-7. *Project settings*

On the next page, click the code icon at the bottom of the page, as shown in Figure 1-8.

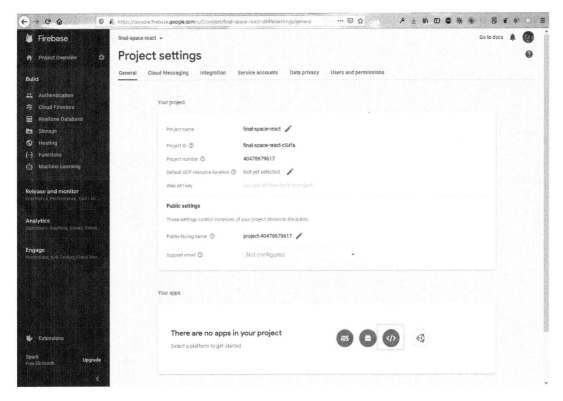

Figure 1-8. *Code icon*

On the next page, enter the same name of the app that you entered earlier, which is **final-space-react** in my case. Also, click the checkbox for Firebase hosting. After that, click the **Register app** button, as shown in Figure 1-9.

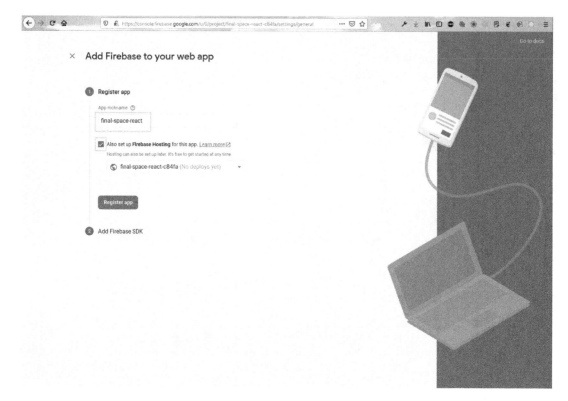

Figure 1-9. *Selecting Firebase hosting*

On the next page, just click the **Next** button (Figure 1-10).

Figure 1-10. *Next button*

On the next page, you will see the command to install `firebase-tools` globally from the terminal (Figure 1-11). So, open any terminal and run the command from anywhere. Notice that this is a one-time setup on a machine, since we are using it with the -g option. The -g option specifies that it needs to be installed globally.

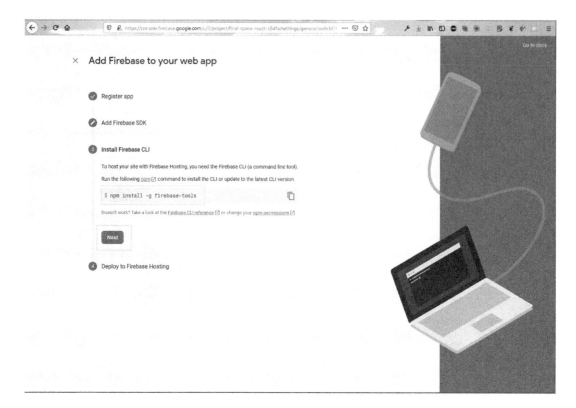

Figure 1-11. *Installing Firebase globally*

Ignore the next set of commands for now and click the **Continue to the console** button (Figure 1-12).

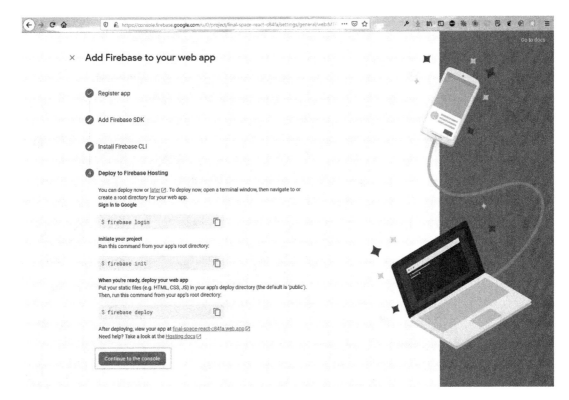

Figure 1-12. *Continuing to the console*

Deploying a Simple ReactJS Project from the Terminal

In this section, you will learn how to deploy a simple ReactJS app that gets data from a simple API. Open `https://github.com/nabendu82/final-space-react` and then click **Code** and the clipboard copy icon (Figure 1-13).

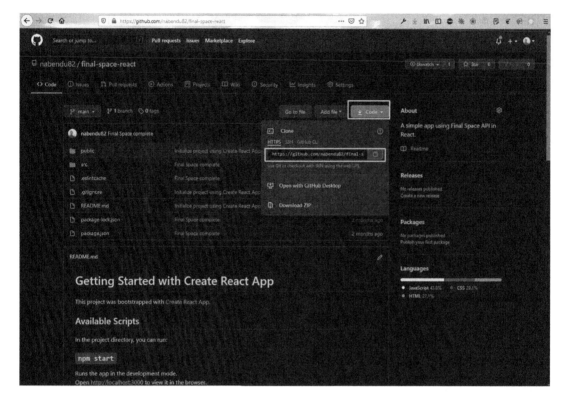

Figure 1-13. *GitHub*

Now, go to any terminal and clone the project using the following command:

```
git clone https://github.com/nabendu82/final-space-react.git
```

After that, change to the project's directory and run `npm i` to install all the dependencies, as shown here:

```
cd final-space-react
npm i
```

Now run `firebase login` from the terminal. If you are running it for the first time, it will give you a pop-up message. After that, run the `firebase init` command. Type Y to proceed (Figure 1-14).

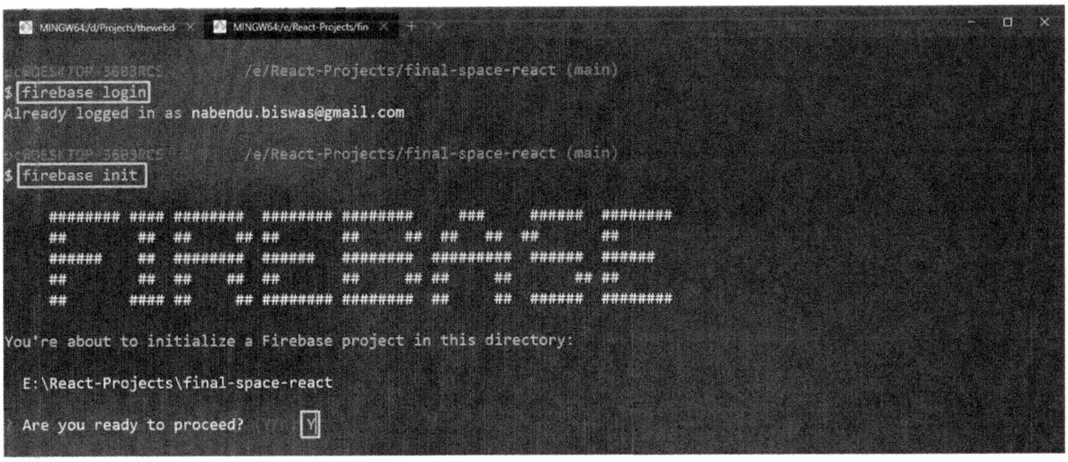

Figure 1-14. *Firebase login*

Next, go down to Hosting using the arrow keys, press the spacebar to select Hosting, and then press Enter, as shown in Figure 1-15.

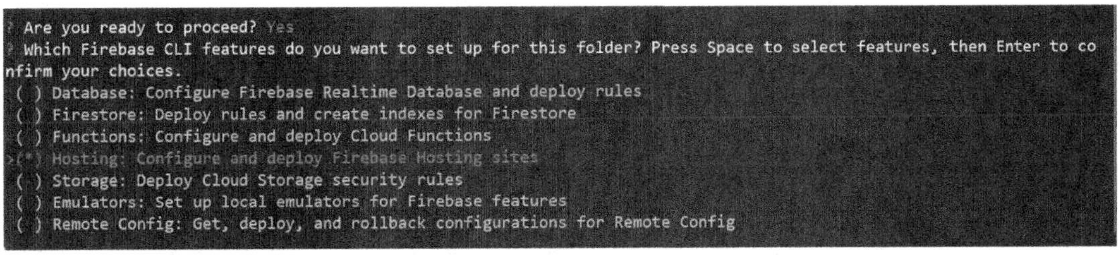

Figure 1-15. *Hosting*

Then select Use an existing project and press Enter, as shown in Figure 1-16.

Figure 1-16. *Existing project*

Here, you need to select the correct project, which is final-space-react-c84fa in my case (Figure 1-17).

```
Please select an option: Use an existing project
Select a default Firebase project for this directory:
facebook-clone-mern-aa5a3 (facebook-clone-mern)
facebook-firebase-clone (facebook-firebase-clone)
final-space-react-c84fa (final-space-react)
homemade-recipes-da051 (homemade-recipes)
instagram-clone-mern-9357c (instagram-clone-mern)
instagram-firebase-clone-110b4 (instagram-firebase-clone)
signal-clone-expo (signal-clone-expo)
```

Figure 1-17. *Selecting the final-space-react project*

Next, choose the public directory, which is build. The next option is Yes for a single-page app and GitHub deploys, where you select No (Figure 1-18).

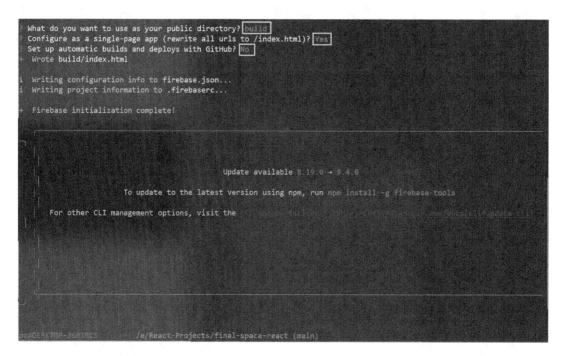

Figure 1-18. *Building the project*

Now, you need to run npm run build in the terminal for a production-optimal build, with this command:

```
npm run build
```

n

The final command is `firebase deploy` to deploy the project to Firebase, as shown here:

```
firebase deploy
```

Now, you can go to `https://final-space-react-c84fa.web.app/` (or adjust to your project name) to see the app running correctly, as shown in Figure 1-19.

Figure 1-19. *Complete app*

Summary

In this chapter, you learned about the awesome Firebase suite of tools from Google. After that you learned how to deploy a React project in Firebase.

CHAPTER 2

Building a To-Do App with React and Firebase

In the previous chapter, you learned to deploy a React app through Firebase. In this chapter, you will learn how to build an awesome to-do list app in ReactJS, with the data stored in the back end, specifically in a Firebase Firestore database. The hosting will also be in Firebase.

We will show how to use Material UI for the icons in the project, and we will be using a useRef hook in this project. Figure 2-1 shows what the app will look like. The user will be able to enter a to-do item and store it in a lovely list in the firebase database. So, this list is permanent and won't be changed after a refresh of browser.

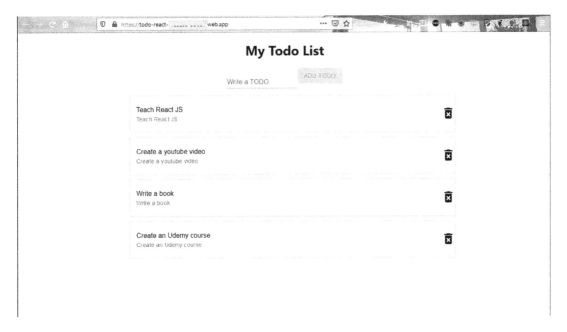

Figure 2-1. *Completed app*

© Nabendu Biswas 2022
N. Biswas, *Beginning React and Firebase*, https://doi.org/10.1007/978-1-4842-7812-3_2

Getting Started

To get started, use the `create-react-app` command to create a new app called `todo-react-firebase`. Specifically, the command for this is as follows:

```
npx create-react-app todo-react-firebase
```

Initial Firebase Setup

Since our front-end site will also be hosted through Firebase, we will create the basic settings while the `create-react-app` command creates our React app. Follow the same steps as in Chapter 1 to set up Firebase.

One additional setup step is required after you click the **Continue to the console** button in the setup procedure. You need to scroll down and click the **Config** radio button and then copy all the data for the `firebaseConfig` section. This is required because we are going to use the Firebase database in our project (Figure 2-2).

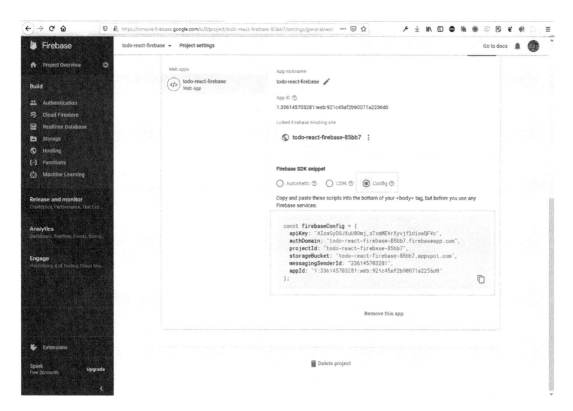

Figure 2-2. *Firebase config*

Now, open the code in VS Code and create a file called `firebase.js` inside the `src` folder. Paste the following code into the file:

```
const firebaseConfig = {
        apiKey: "AIxxxxxxxxxxxxxxxxxxxxxxxxxxxxxxxxxx",
        authDomain: "todo-react-xxxxxxx.firebaseapp.com",
        projectId: "todo-react-xxxxxx",
        storageBucket: "todo-react-xxxxxxxxxxxxxxxxx.com",
        messagingSenderId: "33xxxxxxxxxxx",
        appId: "1:xxxxxxxxxxxx:9xxxxxxxxxxxxx6d0"
};
```

Basic React Setup

Now, we will do the basic setup for ReactJS. Inside the `todo-react-firebase` directory, start the React app with `npm start`. Next, we will delete some of the files because we don't need them. They are actually part of the logo and the other test, which we will not be using in this project. Figure 2-3 shows the files to delete.

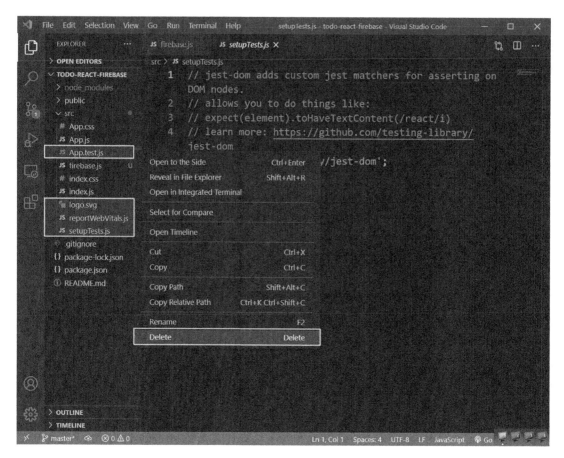

Figure 2-3. *Delete option*

We will remove all the unnecessary boilerplate code, so our `index.js` file will look like this:

```
import React from 'react';
import ReactDOM from 'react-dom';
import './index.css';
import App from './App';

ReactDOM.render(
    <React.StrictMode>
        <App />
    </React.StrictMode>,
    document.getElementById('root')
);
```

The App.js file contains only the "TODO React Firebase" text, as shown here:

```
import './App.css';

function App() {
    return (
        <div className="App">
        <h1>TODO React Firebase</h1>
        </div>
    );
}

export default App;
```

Now, our app will look like Figure 2-4 in localhost.

Figure 2-4. *Localhost app*

Local To-Do List

After doing the setup in the previous section, we will work on our to-do app. We will update our App.js file to contain the logic for a basic to-do list. Here, we are using two state variables: todos and input. We are using the useState hook to declare both of them. todos contains an array containing two strings, and input contains an empty string.

Next, inside the return statement, we use the controlled input of React to update the input of an input box. Next, we have a button and a click event assigned to the button. When we click it, we run a function called addTodo() that changes the state of todos, with setTodos. Here, it appends the already existing content with the user-typed content.

We are using a form to wrap our input and button, and the button type is submit. Therefore, if we type anything in the input box and press Enter on the keyboard, it will work. For that reason, we need to use e.preventDefault() inside the addTodo() function.

```
import { useState } from 'react';
import './App.css';

function App() {
const [todos, setTodos] = useState([
    'Make a react firebase project',
    'Record a coding video'
])

const [input, setInput] = useState('')

const addTodo = e => {
    e.preventDefault()
    setTodos([...todos, input])
    setInput('')
}

return (
    <div className="App">
        <h1>TODO React Firebase</h1>
        <form>
            <input value={input} onChange={e => setInput(e.target.value)}/>
            <button type="submit" onClick={addTodo}>Add Todo</button>
        </form>
        <ul>
            {todos.map(todo => <li>{todo}</li>)}
        </ul>
    </div>
);
}

export default App;
```

Now, in localhost, we will get two items by default, as they are in our initial state of todos. But when we type, we will get new items, as shown in Figure 2-5.

Figure 2-5. *List in localhost*

We will be using Material UI for the icons. So, we need to run two `npm install` commands as per the documentation. We will install `core` and `icons` through the integrated terminal, as shown here:

```
npm install @material-ui/core @material-ui/icons
```

Now, we will use the icons from `material-ui` on our project. We have replaced our Button and Input fields with the `Button` and `Input` from `material-ui`, and we imported them at the top. The updated code is marked in bold here:

```
import { Button, FormControl, Input, InputLabel } from '@material-ui/core';

function App() {
...
...

return (
    <div className="App">
    <h1>TODO React Firebase</h1>
    <form>
            <FormControl>
            <InputLabel>Write a TODO</InputLabel>
            <Input value={input} onChange={e => setInput(e.target.
            value)}/>
            </FormControl>
            <Button type="submit" onClick={addTodo} variant="contained"
            color="primary" disabled={!input}>Add Todo</Button>
    </form>
```

```
    <ul>
            {todos.map(todo => <li>{todo}</li>)}
    </ul>
    </div>
);
}
```

```
export default App;
```

Now, our web app is looking good (Figure 2-6).

Figure 2-6. *The updated web app*

Next, we will move the to-do list to a separate component. So, create a new file called Todo.js inside a components folder. We will send the separate to-do to it as a props. The updated code is shown in bold here:

```
import { Button, FormControl, Input, InputLabel } from '@material-ui/core';
import Todo from './components/Todo';

function App() {
...
...

return (
    <div className="App">
    <h1>TODO React Firebase</h1>
    <form>
    ...
    ...
    </form>
```

```
    <ul>
            {todos.map(todo => <Todo todo={todo} />)}
    </ul>
    </div>
);
}

export default App;
```

Now add the following code into the Todo.js file. We are just using a bunch of material-ui icons and showing the props called todo. These icons help us to make the list item prettier.

```
import { List, ListItem, ListItemAvatar, ListItemText } from
'@material-ui/core'
import React from 'react'

const Todo = ({ todo }) => {
    return (
        <List className="todo__list">
            <ListItem>
                <ListItemAvatar />
                <ListItemText primary={todo} secondary={todo} />
            </ListItem>
        </List>
    )
}

export default Todo
```

Now, in localhost, we will be able to see these changes, and our list will be looking good (Figure 2-7).

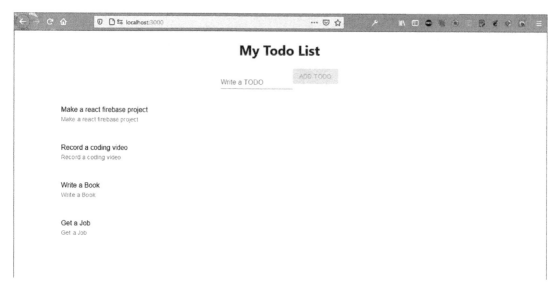

Figure 2-7. *Todo list*

Now, it's time to hook up Firebase to the project.

Using Firebase

Now, we will start setting up Firebase for the back end. For that we will first install all dependencies for Firebase in the terminal by running the following command:

```
npm i firebase
```

Next, we will update our `firebase.js` file to use the config to initialize the app. After that, we use Firestore as the database. The updated code is highlighted in bold here:

```
import firebase from 'firebase'

const firebaseConfig = {
    ...
    ...
};

const firebaseApp = firebase.initializeApp(firebaseConfig)
const db = firebaseApp.firestore()

export { db }
```

Now, we will go back to Firebase and click **Cloud Firestore** and then click the **Create database** button, as shown in Figure 2-8.

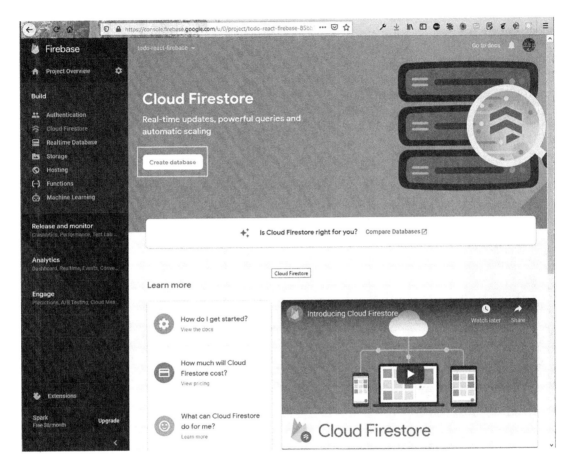

Figure 2-8. *Creating the database*

On the next screen, select **Start in test mode** and then click the **Next** button, as shown in Figure 2-9.

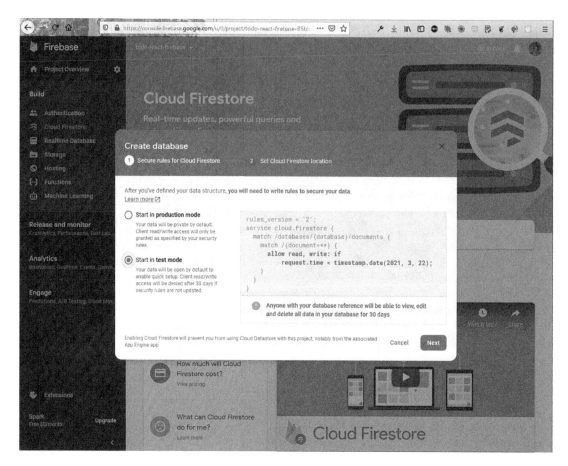

Figure 2-9. *Test mode*

On the next screen, click the **Enable** button (Figure 2-10).

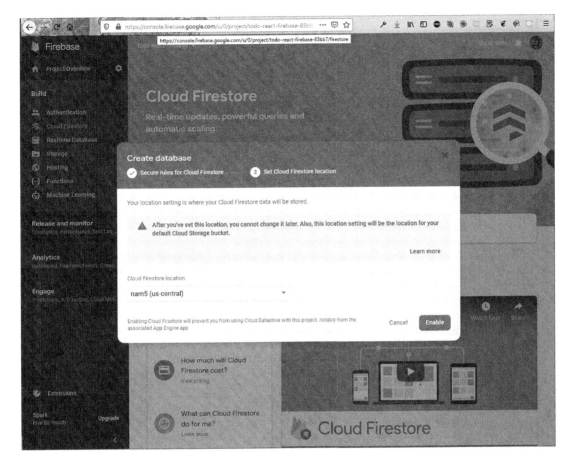

Figure 2-10. *Enable button*

On the next screen, click **Start collection**, as shown in Figure 2-11.

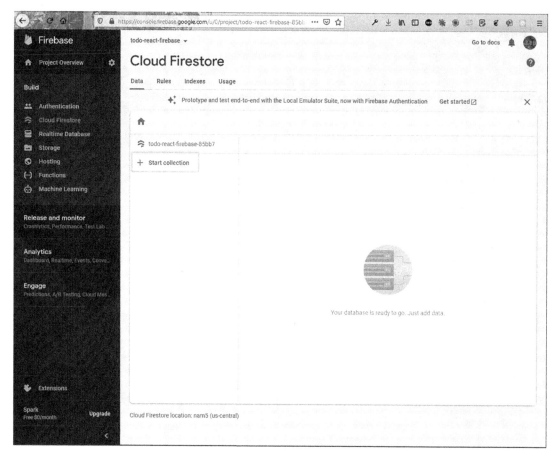

Figure 2-11. *Starting the collection*

It will open the pop-up shown in Figure 2-12. We need to enter **todos** in the
Collection ID field and click the Next button.

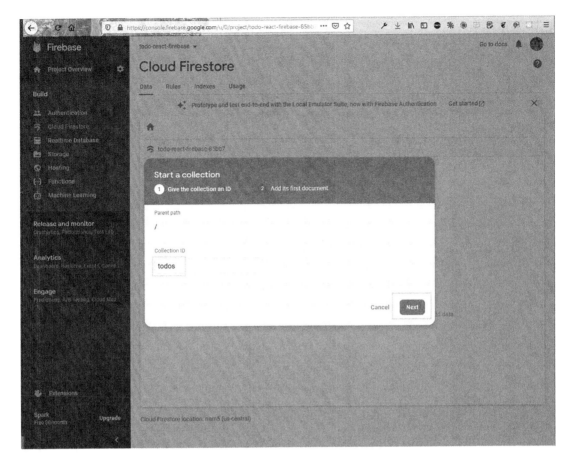

Figure 2-12. *The to-dos*

On the next screen, fill the Document ID field by clicking **Auto ID**. Also enter **todo** in the Field field. After that, click the **Save** button (Figure 2-13).

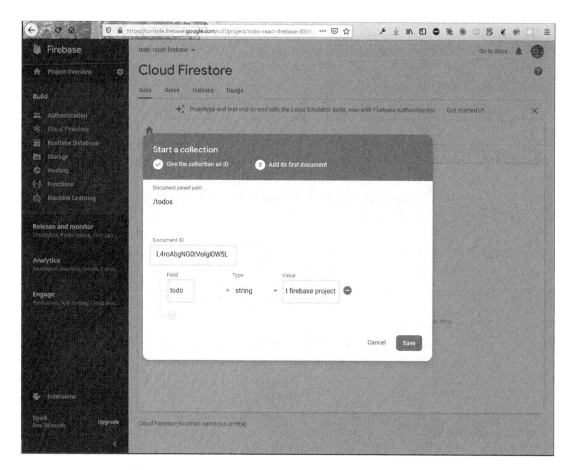

Figure 2-13. *Fields*

That will take us back to the main screen. Now click the **Add document** link. This will again open the same pop-up, where we will add the details of another to-do item. Now, we have two to-dos in our database (Figure 2-14).

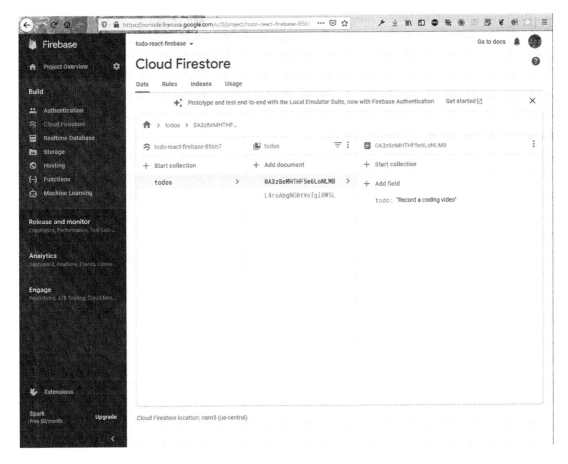

Figure 2-14. *Two to-dos*

Adding Firebase to the App

Now we are going to remove the hard-coded to-dos in App.js and use the data from the Firebase database. So, go back to App.js and remove the hard-coded stuff in the useState code for todos. We have also created the required imports.

After that, within useEffect, we are calling the collection todos, and then we take the snapshot. In Firebase terms, it is the live data, which we will get instantly. We will then set this data in the todos array, via setTodos().

Also, notice that useEffect has input inside the array. So, any time a todo is added by the user, it will instantly display in our app.

Also, notice that we have changed the way we loop through data, using todos. This is done because we receive the data as an array of objects. The updated code is shown in bold here:

```
import { useState, useEffect } from 'react';
import Todo from './components/Todo';
import { db } from './firebase';

function App() {
const [todos, setTodos] = useState([])
const [input, setInput] = useState('')
useEffect(() => {
  db.collection('todos').onSnapshot(snapshot => {
    setTodos(snapshot.docs.map(doc => doc.data()))
  })
}, [input])

...
...
return (
    <div className="App">
    <h1>TODO React Firebase</h1>
        ...
        ...
    <ul>
    {todos.map(({ todo }) => <Todo todo={todo} />)}
    </ul>
    </div>
);
}

export default App;
```

Now, we will add the functionality so the user can add the to-do item. For this we just need to add the input to the collection, using add(). Also, notice that we are adding the server timestamp, while adding a to-do. We are doing this because we need to order the to-dos in descending order. The updated code is marked in bold here:

```
import { db } from './firebase';
import firebase from 'firebase';

function App() {
const [todos, setTodos] = useState([])
const [input, setInput] = useState('')
useEffect(() => {
  db.collection('todos').orderBy('timestamp','desc').onSnapshot
  (snapshot => {
    setTodos(snapshot.docs.map(doc => doc.data()))
  })
}, [input])

const addTodo = e => {
    e.preventDefault()
    db.collection('todos').add({
    todo: input,
    timestamp: firebase.firestore.FieldValue.serverTimestamp()
    })
    setInput('')
}
...
...
```

Now, we need to delete the old collection in Firebase, because none of the records has a timestamp (Figure 2-15).

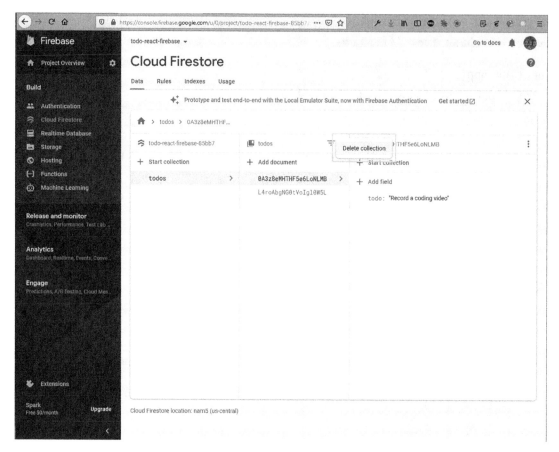

Figure 2-15. *Deleting the collection*

It will also display a pop-up to confirm this (Figure 2-16).

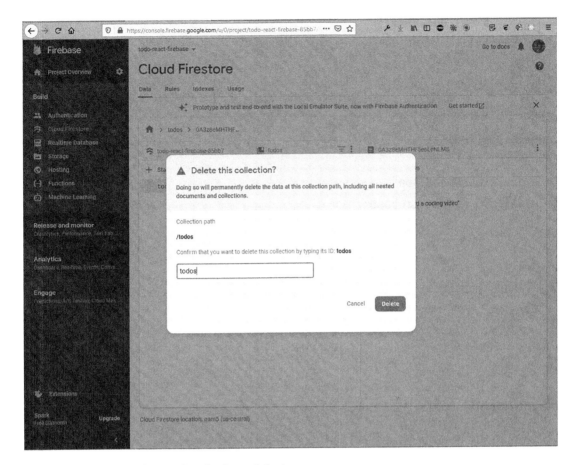

Figure 2-16. *Confirmation before deleting*

Now, we also want to get the ID of each item that we require for the key and also for deleting, which we are going to implement. The key is essential in React for optimization, and we also get a warning in the console. So, we need to change the structure in which we set the data in `setTodos()`.

Now, we are mapping through it in a different way, specifically when we are passing the single item to a `Todo` component. Here's the updated code:

```
function App() {
...
useEffect(() => {
  db.collection('todos').orderBy('timestamp','desc').onSnapshot(snapshot => {
        setTodos(snapshot.docs.map(doc => ({
        id: doc.id,
```

```
            item: doc.data()
            })))
    })
}, [input])

...
console.log(todos);
return (
    <div className="App">
    <h1>TODO React Firebase</h1>
            ...
            ...
    <ul>
    {todos.map(it => <Todo key={it.id} arr={it} />)}
    </ul>
    </div>
);
}

export default App;
```

Now, in the Todo.js file, we are getting a different structure, and we are updating our file for that.

We have also added the delete functionality, in which we have to get the ID of the item and call the delete(). The updated code is marked in bold here:

```
import { db } from '../firebase'
import DeleteForeverIcon from '@material-ui/icons/DeleteForever'

const Todo = ({ arr }) => {
        return (
        <List className="todo__list">
        <ListItem>
                    <ListItemAvatar />
                    <ListItemText
                     primary={arr.item.todo}
                     secondary={arr.item.todo}
                     />
```

```
    </ListItem>
    <DeleteForeverIcon
          onClick={() => {db.collection('todos').doc(arr.id).delete()}}
    />
    </List>
    )
}
```

```
export default Todo
```

Now, in localhost, we can add and delete any item. Also, notice the structure in the console log (Figure 2-17).

Figure 2-17. *Console log*

We are done with the app, and only the styling remains. Let's make it prettier now. In the App.js file, change className to app. The updated code is marked in bold here:

```
return (
    <div className="app">
    ...
    </div>
);
}

export default App;
```

Next, in the App.css file, remove everything and insert the content shown here:

```
.app {
    display:grid;
    place-items: center;
}
```

Now, in the Todo.js file, add the import for the Todo.css file. Also, set fontSize to large for the Delete icon. The updated code is marked in bold here:

```
import './Todo.css'

const Todo = ({ arr }) => {
    return (
    <List className="todo__list">

            ...

    <DeleteForeverIcon fontSize='large'
            onClick={() => {db.collection('todos').doc(arr.id).delete()}}
    />
    </List>
    )
}
```

Next, in the Todo.css file, add the following content:

```
.todo__list{
    display:flex;
    justify-content: center;
    align-items: center;
    width: 800px;
    border: 1px solid lightgray;
    margin-bottom: 10px !important;
}
```

Now, in localhost, the app is looking perfect (Figure 2-18).

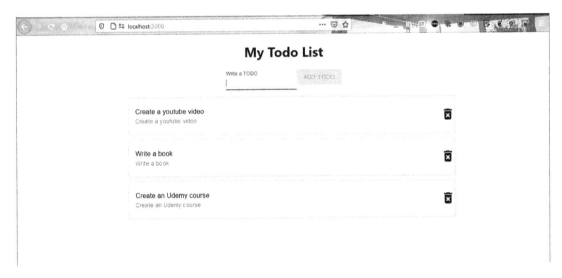

Figure 2-18. *Our app after adding the styling*

Deploying Firebase

To deploy the app, we will follow the same steps as in Chapter 1. After doing that, we can see that the app was successfully deployed from the terminal (Figure 2-19).

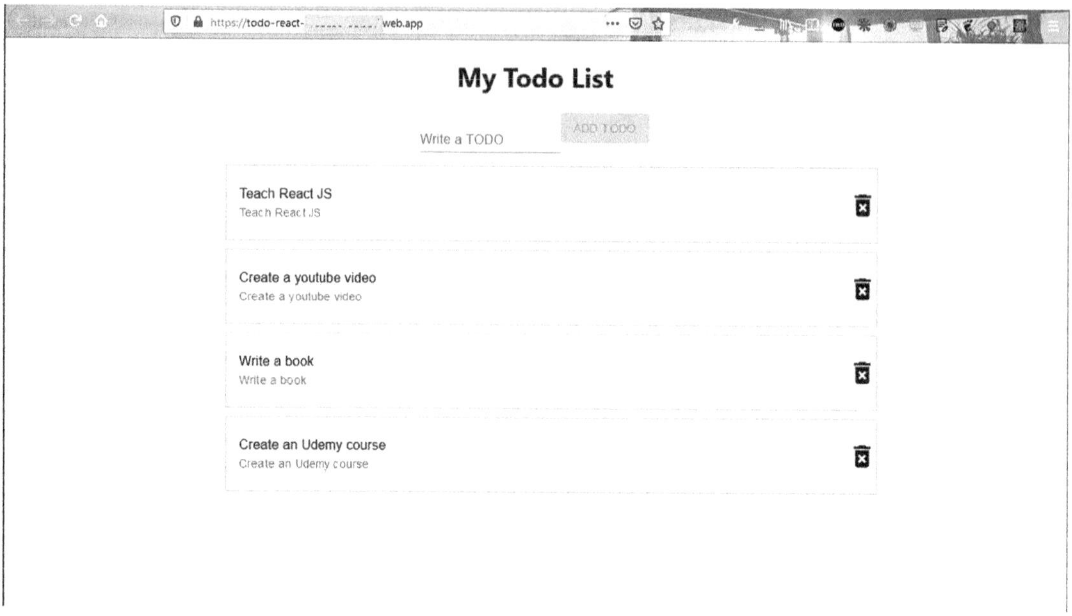

Figure 2-19. *The completed app*

Summary

In this chapter, you created a beautiful to-do app. The data for the app was stored in a Firebase Firestore database, and it even has delete functionality.

CHAPTER 3

Building a Stories App with React and Firebase

In this chapter, you will learn how to build a stories app in ReactJS. Stories apps are quite popular nowadays, and every big social media platform has the capability for users to add *stories*, which are short videos, to their platforms. In our app, we will be able to scroll short videos that will be stored in the Firebase Firestore database. The final app will look like Figure 3-1.

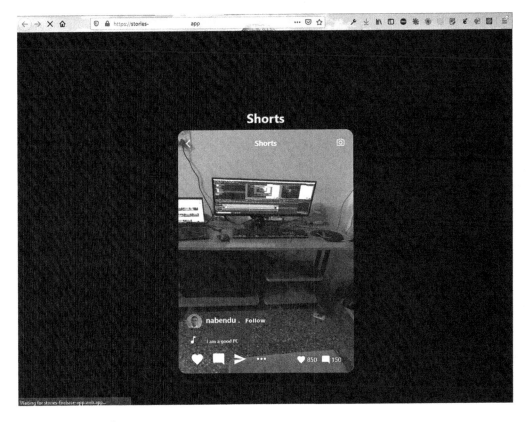

Figure 3-1. *Final app in use*

© Nabendu Biswas 2022
N. Biswas, *Beginning React and Firebase*, https://doi.org/10.1007/978-1-4842-7812-3_3

The hosting and the database will be in Firebase. We will also be using Material UI for the icons in the project.

So, use the `create-react-app` command to create a new app called `stories-firebase-app`. Specifically, open any terminal and run the following command:

```
npx create-react-app stories-firebase-app
```

Initial Firebase Setup

Since our front-end site will also be hosted through Firebase, we will create the basic settings while the `create-react-app` command creates our React app. Go ahead and follow the steps listed in Chapter 1 to create the app. I have created an app named `stories-firebase-app` (Figure 3-2).

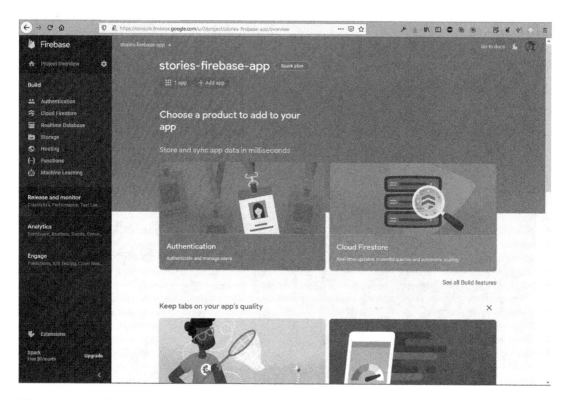

Figure 3-2. *Creating the app*

Now, click the **Settings** icon at the top-left corner of the screen. After that, click the **Project settings** button (Figure 3-3).

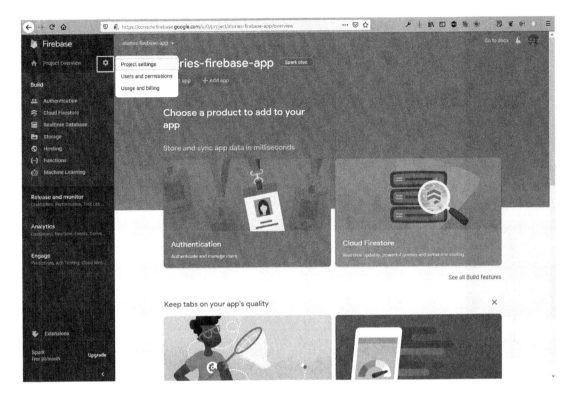

Figure 3-3. *Settings*

Now, scroll down, click the **Config** radio button, and then copy all the code for the firebaseConfig section (Figure 3-4).

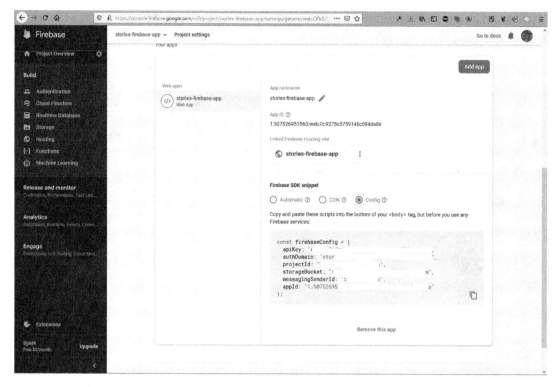

Figure 3-4. *. firebaseConfig code*

Basic React Setup

Our React setup should be completed by this time. So, go back to the terminal and `cd` into the newly created `stories-firebase-app` directory.

After that, open the directory in VS Code, create a file called `firebase.js` inside the `src` folder, and paste the content from the previous Firebase screen there. The code is shown here:

```
const firebaseConfig = {
        apiKey: "AIxxxxxxxxxxxxxxxxxxxxxxxxxxxxxKT4",
        authDomain: "stories-xxxxxx.xxxxxxxx.com",
        projectId: "stories-xxxxxx",
        storageBucket: "stories-fxxxxxxxx.com",
        messagingSenderId: "50xxxxxxxx63",
        appId: "1:507xxxxxxx63:web:0c9xxxxxxxxxxda8e"
};
```

In the `stories-firebase-app` directory, start the React app with `npm start`. Next, we will delete some of the files, as shown in Figure 3-5, because we don't need them.

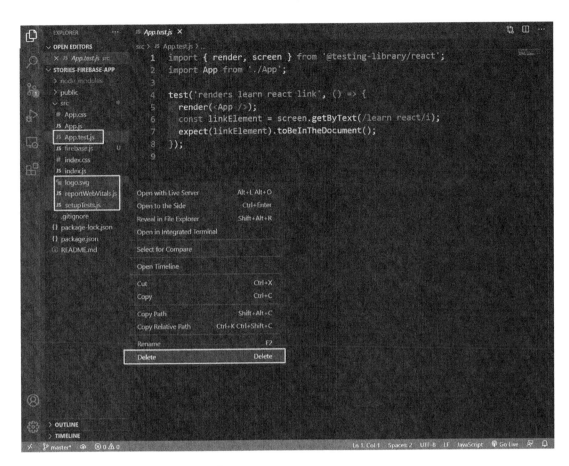

Figure 3-5. *Deleting some code*

We will remove all the unnecessary boilerplate code, so our `index.js` file will look like this:

```
import React from 'react';
import ReactDOM from 'react-dom';
import './index.css';
import App from './App';

ReactDOM.render(
    <React.StrictMode>
        <App />
```

```
    </React.StrictMode>,
    document.getElementById('root')
);
```

The `App.js` file contains only the "Stories app React" text. We have removed all the other content from the `App.css` file. The updated code for the `App.css` file is shown here:

```
import './App.css';

function App() {
    return (
        <div className="app">
        <h1>Stories app React</h1>
        </div>
    );
}
export default App;
```

In the `index.css` file, update the CSS to use `margin: 0` throughout. Specifically, add the following code at the top:

```
* {
  margin: 0;
}
```

Basic Structure of the App

We will now create the basic structure in our app. So, update `App.js` with the following content. We are adding the image and heading first. Here, we have created two `div`s: `app__top` and `app__videos`. Now, the `app__top` contains an image and an `h1`.

```
import './App.css';

function App() {
    return (
        <div className="app">
        <div className="app__top">
            <img src="logo192.png" alt="App Logo" className=
            "app__logo"/>
```

```
        <h1>Shorts</h1>
      </div>
      <div className="app__videos">

      </div>
      </div>
    );
}
export default App;
```

Next, we will add new content in the App.css file. Here, we are placing everything in the center using a grid. We also have a style of scroll-snap-type: y mandatory at two places. It is used to give the scroll feature in our app for smooth scrolling.

```
html{
    scroll-snap-type: y mandatory;
}

.app{
    display: grid;
    place-items: center;
    height: 100vh;
    background-color: black;
}

.app__top {
    margin-bottom: -150px;
}
.app__top > h1 {
    text-align: center;
    color: white;
}

.app__logo {
    height: 12vh;
}
```

```
.app__videos {
    position:relative;
    height: 65vh;
    background-color: white;
    width: 70%;
    border-radius: 20px;
    max-width: 450px;
    max-height: 1200px;
    overflow: scroll;
    scroll-snap-type: y mandatory;
}

.app__videos::-webkit-scrollbar{
    display: none;
}

.app__videos{
    -ms-overflow-style: none;
    scrollbar-width: none;
}
```

Now, our app will look like Figure 3-6 in localhost.

Figure 3-6. *App outline*

Showing Short Videos in the App

After setting up the basic layout in the previous section, we will now start creating the
functionality to show short videos in our app.

To start, create a components folder inside the src folder and create two files called
VideoCard.js and VideoCard.css inside the src folder.

Next, in the VideoCard.js file, put the video tag and a vertical video link. I copied
the link from a short YouTube video on my channel.

```
import React from 'react'
import './VideoCard.css'

const VideoCard = () => {
    return (
```

```
        <div className="videoCard">
            <video
                src="https://res.cloudinary.com/dxkxvfo2o/video/upload/
                v1608169738/video1_cvrjfm.mp4"
                className="videoCard__player"
                alt="Short Video App"
                loop
            />
        </div>
    )
}

export default VideoCard
```

Now, we will add the following code in the `VideoCard.css` file. Here, we again need to add `scroll-snap-align: start` to have the smooth scroll feature in the videos.

```
.videoCard{
    position: relative;
    background-color: white;
    width: 100%;
    height:100%;
    scroll-snap-align: start;
}

.videoCard__player{
    object-fit: fill;
    width: 100%;
    height: 100%;
}
```

Now, in `App.js`, add two `VideoCard` components, because we are need more than one video to see the snapping feature. The updated code is shown in bold here:

```
import './App.css';
import VideoCard from './components/VideoCard';

function App() {
        return (
```

```
        <div className="app">
        <div className="app__top">

                ...
        </div>
        <div className="app__videos">
                <VideoCard />
                <VideoCard />
         </div>
        </div>
        );
}
export default App;
```

Now, videos are showing perfectly with the snapping feature (Figure 3-7).

Figure 3-7. *Video snapping*

Right now our videos don't play, because we have not implemented the onClick functionality. To make them play, we will need to use a reference (or *ref*). A ref is required because we will be implementing the pause and play functions for when the user clicks the mouse on the screen. We will first import the useRef and useState hooks, and then we will add a videoRef variable. We are using videoRef inside the video element, where we also created an onClick handler that fires the function handleVideoPress.

Inside the handleVideoPress function, we are using a state variable called playing to check whether the video is playing. We are setting it to pause with videoRef.current. pause() and also changing the playing state to false. We are doing the reverse in the else part. The updated code is marked in bold here:

```
import React, { useRef, useState } from 'react'
import './VideoCard.css'

const VideoCard = () => {
    const [playing, setPlaying] = useState(false)
    const videoRef = useRef(null)

    const handleVideoPress = () => {
    if(playing){
        videoRef.current.pause()
        setPlaying(false)
    } else {
        videoRef.current.play()
        setPlaying(true)
    }
    }

    return (
    <div className="videoCard">
        <video
        ...
        loop
        ref={videoRef}
        onClick={handleVideoPress}
        />
    </div>
```

```
        )
}
export default VideoCard
```

Now, in localhost, just click the video and it will play. Click again to pause it.

Creating the Header Component

We will be using Material UI for the icons, which we will use next. So, we need to do two npm installs per the documentation. We will install core and icons through the terminal by using the following command:

```
npm i @material-ui/core @material-ui/icons
```

We will now create the header for our video component. So, create files called VideoHeader.js and VideoHeader.css inside the components folder.

```
import React from 'react'
import './VideoHeader.css'

const VideoHeader = () => {
        return (
        <div className="videoHeader">

        </div>
        )
}
export default VideoHeader
```

Now, in the VideoHeader.js file, put the following content. Here, we are using material-ui to show two icons: ArrowBackIos and CameraAltOutlined. The updated content is marked as bold here:

```
import React from 'react'
import './VideoHeader.css'
import ArrowBackIosIcon from '@material-ui/icons/ArrowBackIos'
import CameraAltOutlinedIcon from '@material-ui/icons/CameraAltOutlined'
```

```
const VideoHeader = () => {
    return (
        <div className="videoHeader">
            <ArrowBackIosIcon />
            <h3>Shorts</h3>
            <CameraAltOutlinedIcon />
        </div>
    )
}

export default VideoHeader
```

Next, we will style these in the VideoHeader.css file.

```
.videoHeader {
    display: flex;
    justify-content: space-between;
    align-items: center;
    position: absolute;
    width: 100%;
    color: white;
}

.videoHeader > * {
    padding: 20px;
}
```

Now, include this VideoHeader component in the VideoCard.js file. The updated content is marked as bold here:

```
import VideoHeader from './VideoHeader'

const VideoCard = () => {
    ...
    ...
    return (
    <div className="videoCard">
            <VideoHeader />
```

```
            <video
                    ...
            />
    </div>
    )
}
```

```
export default VideoCard
```

Now, in localhost we see our nice header component (Figure 3-8).

Figure 3-8. *Header*

Creating the Footer Component

We will now create a footer for our video component. The footer component will show some icons in the footer of the app. So, create two files called VideoFooter.js and VideoFooter.css inside the components folder.

Also, we are doing a bit of optimization by passing props from the App.js file in the VideoCard component. We are passing two different set of props, in two VideoCard components. The updated content is marked in bold here:

```
import './App.css';
import VideoCard from './components/VideoCard';

function App() {
        return (
        <div className="app">
        <div className="app__top">

                ...

        </div>
        <div className="app__videos">
        <VideoCard
                url="https://res.cloudinary.com/dxkxvfo2o/video/upload/
                v1608169738/video1_cvrjfm.mp4"
                channel="TWD"
                avatarSrc="https://pbs.twimg.com/profile_
                images/1020939891457241088/fcbu814K_400x400.jpg"
                song="I am a Windows PC"
                likes={950}
                shares={200}
        />
        <VideoCard
                url="https://res.cloudinary.com/dxkxvfo2o/video/upload/
                v1608169739/video2_mecbdo.mp4"
                channel="nabendu"
                avatarSrc="https://pbs.twimg.com/profile_
                images/1020939891457241088/fcbu814K_400x400.jpg"
                song="I am a good PC"
```

```
                likes={850}
                shares={150}
       />
       </div>
       </div>
      );
}
export default App;
```

Then in the VideoCard.js file, we will first use the prop called url in video. Also, call the new VideoFooter component, where we will pass the rest of the props. The updated content is marked in bold here:

```
import VideoFooter from './VideoFooter'
import VideoHeader from './VideoHeader'

const VideoCard = ({ url, channel, avatarSrc, song, likes, shares }) => {
    ...
    ...
       return (
       <div className="videoCard">
                <VideoHeader />
                <video
                src={url}
                className="videoCard__player"
                alt="Short Video App"
                loop
                ref={videoRef}
                onClick={handleVideoPress}
                />
                <VideoFooter
                channel={channel}
                likes={likes}
                shares={shares}
                avatarSrc={avatarSrc}
                song={song}
```

```
                  />
      </div>
    )
}

export default VideoCard
```

Now, our VideoFooter.js file will contain the following content. We are using the channel and avatarSrc props and showing an avatar and a channel name.

```
import React from 'react'
import './VideoFooter.css'
import { Button, Avatar } from '@material-ui/core'

const VideoFooter = ({ channel, avatarSrc, song, likes, shares }) => {
    return (
        <div className='videoFooter'>
            <div className="videoFooter__text">
                <Avatar src={avatarSrc} />
                <h3>
                    {channel} . <Button>Follow</Button>
                </h3>
            </div>
        </div>
    )
}

export default VideoFooter
```

Next, we will add the styles for these in the VideoFooter.css file.

```
.videoFooter__text{
    position: absolute;
    bottom: 0;
    color: white;
    display: flex;
    margin-bottom: 20px;
}
```

```
.videoFooter__text > h3 {
    margin-left: 10px;
    padding-bottom: 20px;
}

.videoFooter__text > h3 > button {
    color: white;
    font-weight: 900;
    text-transform: inherit;
}
```

Now, in localhost we will start setting the footer component (Figure 3-9).

Figure 3-9. *Footer*

Now, let's create a nice ticker in our project. For that we will install a package called react-ticker in our project. This package allows us to show moving text, like a news feed. We can use the integrated terminal to do the installation with the following command:

```
npm i react-ticker
```

Next, we will include Ticker as per the documentation, along with MusicNoteIcon, in our VideoFooter.js file, as shown here:

```
import MusicNoteIcon from '@material-ui/icons/MusicNote'
import Ticker from 'react-ticker'

const VideoFooter = ({ channel, avatarSrc, song, likes, shares }) => {
    return (
    <div className='videoFooter'>
    <div className="videoFooter__text">

            ..
    </div>
    <div className="videoFooter__ticker">
                <MusicNoteIcon className="videoFooter__icon" />
                <Ticker mode="smooth">
                {(({ index }) => (
                <>
                <h1>{song}</h1>
                </>
                )}
                </Ticker>
    </div>
    </div>
    )
}

export default VideoFooter
```

Next, we will include the following styles in the VideoFooter.css file:

```
.videoFooter{
    position: relative;
    bottom: 100px;
    margin-left: 20px;
}

.videoFooter__ticker > .ticker{
    height: fit-content;
    margin-left: 30px;
    margin-bottom: 20px;
    width: 60%;
}

.videoFooter__ticker h1{
    padding-top: 7px;
    font-size: 12px;
    color: white;
}

.videoFooter__icon{
    position: absolute;
    left: 5px;
    color: white;
}
```

Now, we will see this nice ticker scrolling across our screen in localhost (Figure 3-10).

Figure 3-10. *Ticker*

Now, we will add some remaining elements in the VideoFooter.js file to finish our app. Here, we are adding some more icons and using the likes and shares props:

```
import Ticker from 'react-ticker'
import { Favorite, ModeComment, MoreHoriz, Send } from '@material-ui/icons'

const VideoFooter = ({ channel, avatarSrc, song, likes, shares }) => {
    return (
    <div className='videoFooter'>
            <div className="videoFooter__text">
                ...
            </div>
            <div className="videoFooter__ticker">
                ...
```

```
            </div>
            <div className="videoFooter__actions">
            <div className="videoFooter__actionsLeft">
            <Favorite fontSize="large" />
            <ModeComment fontSize="large" />
            <Send fontSize="large" />
            <MoreHoriz fontSize="large" />
            </div>
            <div className="videoFooter__actionsRight">
            <div className="videoFooter__stat">
                    <Favorite />
                    <p>{likes}</p>
            </div>
            <div className="videoFooter__stat">
                    <ModeComment />
                    <p>{shares}</p>
            </div>
            </div>
            </div>
        </div>
        )
}

export default VideoFooter
```

Next, we will add some new styles in the VideoFooter.css file, as shown here:

```
.videoFooter__actions{
    display: flex;
    position: absolute;
    width: 95%;
    color: white;
    justify-content: space-between;
}

.videoFooter__actionsLeft > .MuiSvgIcon-root{
    padding: 0 10px;
}
```

```
.videoFooter__actionsRight{
    display: flex;
}

.videoFooter__stat{
    display: flex;
    align-items: center;
    margin-right: 10px;
}

.videoFooter__stat > p{
    margin-left: 3px;
}
```

Now, our app is complete with the additional elements we just added (Figure 3-11).

Figure 3-11. *App complete*

Setting Up the Firebase Database

We will now be setting up Firebase. The first thing to do is install Firebase in our project by running the following command from the terminal:

```
npm i firebase
```

Next, we will update our firebase.js file to use the config to initialize the app. After that, we can use Firestore as the database. The updated content for this is marked in bold here:

```
import firebase from 'firebase';

const firebaseConfig = {
    ...
};

const firebaseApp = firebase.initializeApp(firebaseConfig)
const db = firebaseApp.firestore()

export default db
```

Now, we will go back to Firebase and click Cloud Firestore and then the **Create database** button (Figure 3-12).

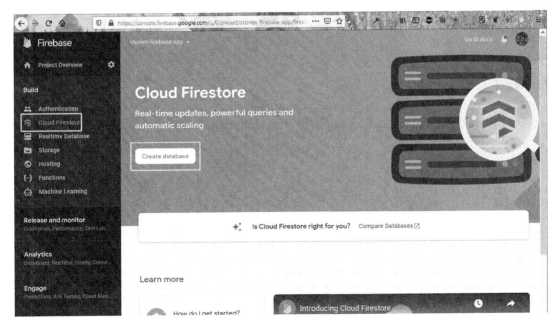

Figure 3-12.   *Creating a database*

On the next screen, select **Start in test mode** and then click the **Next** button (Figure 3-13).

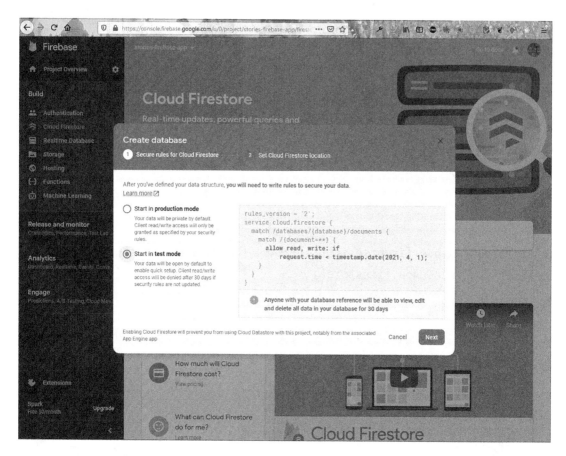

Figure 3-13. *Test mode*

On the next screen, click the **Enable** button (Figure 3-14).

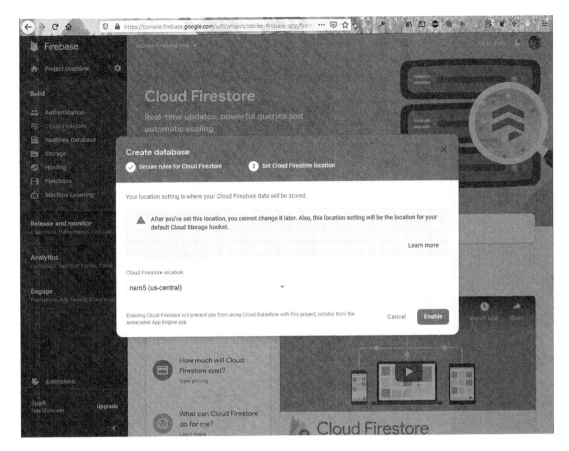

Figure 3-14. *Enable button*

On the next screen, click **Start collection** (Figure 3-15).

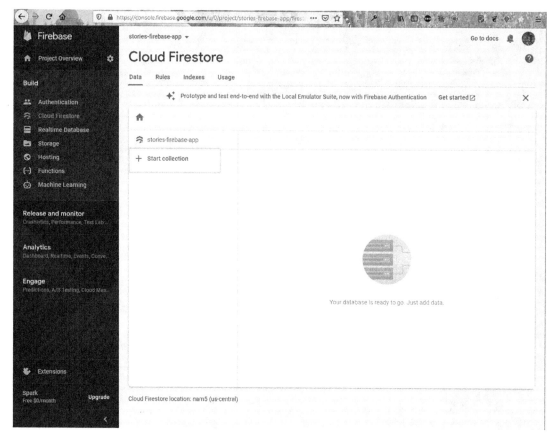

Figure 3-15. *Starting the collection*

This will open the pop-up shown in Figure 3-16. We need to give the collection ID, so enter **videos** in the Collection ID field and then click the **Next** button.

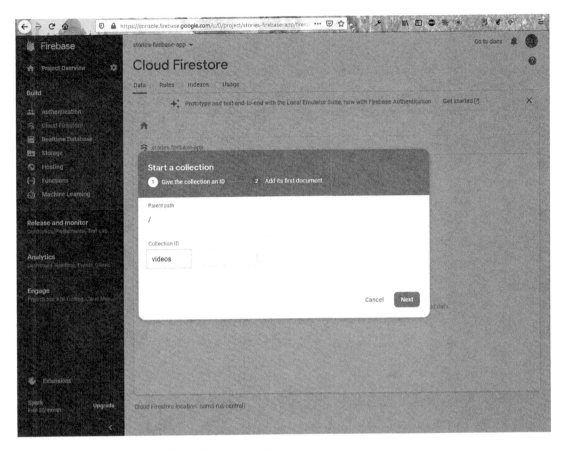

Figure 3-16. *Entering the collection ID*

On the next screen, create the document ID by clicking **Auto ID**. Also add the fields **url**, **channel**, **avatarSrc**, **song**, **likes**, and **shares**. Put all the values from the App.js file in the Value fields. Also, note that the likes, shares, and messages are the number type and the rest are the string type. After that, click the **Save** button (Figure 3-17).

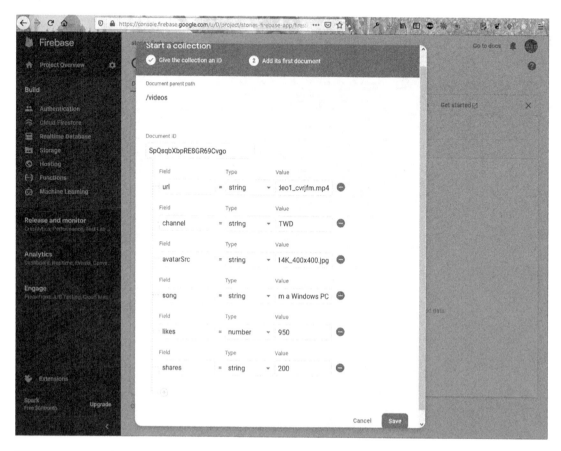

Figure 3-17. *Creating a collection*

This will take us back to the main screen. Now click the **Add document** link. This will again open the same pop-up we saw earlier, where we will add the details of another video from the App.js file (Figure 3-18).

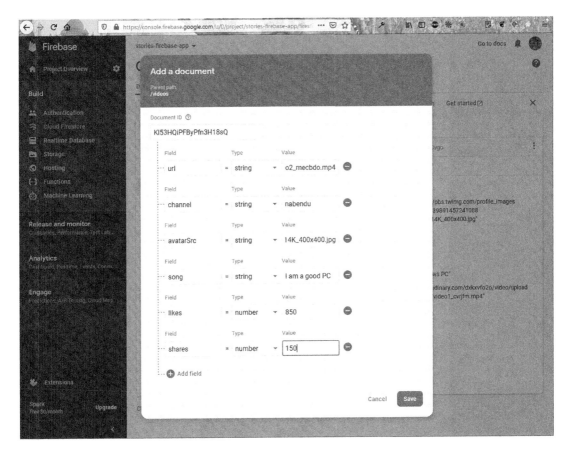

Figure 3-18. *Another collection*

Now, we have two videos in our database (Figure 3-19).

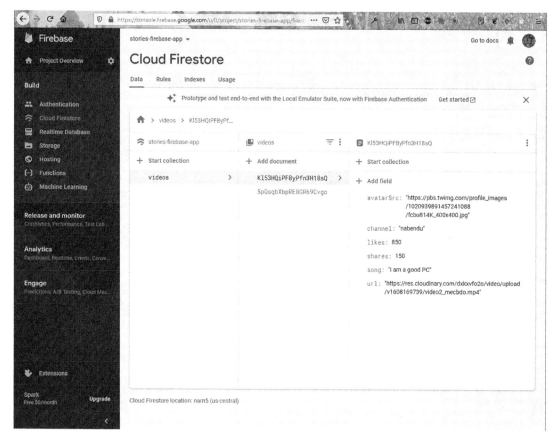

Figure 3-19. *Two videos*

Integrating the Firebase Database with React

Now, go back to App.js and create a new state called videos using the useState hook. We will then map over it and pass the parameters to the VideoCard component. Notice that we have removed the hard-coded stuff, as we will not get this data from the database. The updated content is marked in bold here:

```
import { useState } from 'react';
import './App.css';
import VideoCard from './components/VideoCard';

function App() {
  const [videos, setVideos] = useState([])
```

```
  return (
        <div className="app">
        <div className="app__top">
        ...
        </div>
        <div className="app__videos">
                {videos.map((({ url, channel, avatarSrc, song, likes,
                shares }) => (
                <VideoCard
                        url={url}
                        channel={channel}
                        avatarSrc={avatarSrc}
                        song={song}
                        likes={likes}
                        shares={shares}
                />
                ))}
        </div>
        </div>
  );
}
export default App;
```

Now, we will use the data stored in the local Firebase file in our app. After that, within useEffect, we are calling the collection videos and then taking a snapshot. In Firebase terms, this is the live data, which we will get instantly. We will then set this data in a video array, via setVideos().

Also, notice that useEffect has videos inside the array. So, anytime a new video is added in the Firebase database, it will instantly display in our app. The updated content is marked in bold here:

```
import { useEffect, useState } from 'react';
import './App.css';
import VideoCard from './components/VideoCard';
import db from './firebase';
```

```
function App() {
  const [videos, setVideos] = useState([])

  useEffect(() => {
    db.collection('videos').onSnapshot(snapshot => {
      setVideos(snapshot.docs.map(doc => doc.data()))
    })
  }, [videos])

  return (
  ...
  )
```

Now, our app is complete, and we are getting the data from the Firebase back end (Figure 3-20).

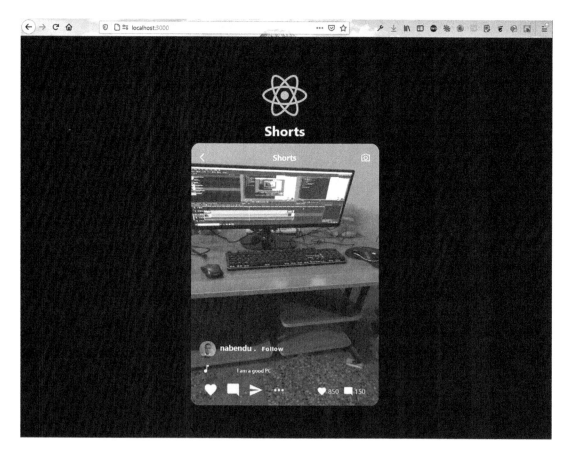

Figure 3-20. *Getting data from database*

Deploying and Hosting Through Firebase

Now, we can deploy our app in Firebase. We just follow the same steps as described earlier.

The deployment was successful, and our app is working properly (Figure 3-21).

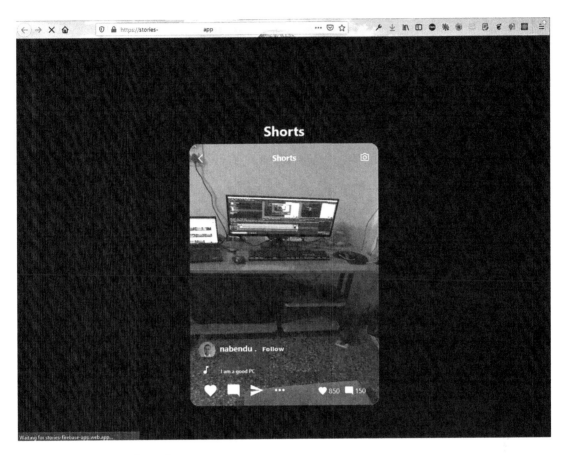

Figure 3-21. *Deployed app*

Summary

In this chapter, you learned how to create a stories video app. The data for the app is stored in the Firebase Firestore database, and it also has a nice scroll feature.

CHAPTER 4

Building a Storage App with React and Firebase

Welcome to a new ReactJS project, where we are going to build a storage app in ReactJS. Storage apps are used to store your data in the cloud as a backup. There are many popular storage apps such as Dropbox and Google Drive.

The hosting and the database will be in Firebase. The login of the app will be through Google Authentication. We will also be using Material UI for the icons in the project. The final project will look like Figure 4-1.

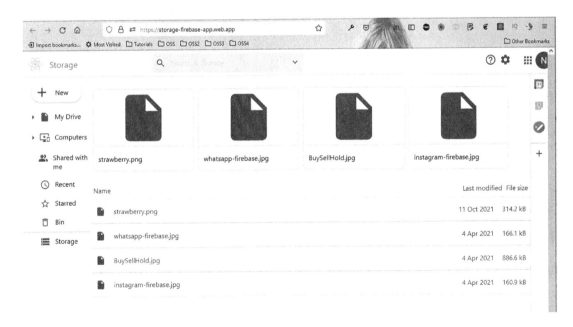

Figure 4-1. Completed project

© Nabendu Biswas 2022
N. Biswas, *Beginning React and Firebase*, https://doi.org/10.1007/978-1-4842-7812-3_4

Getting Started

Use the `create-react-app` command to create a new app called `storage-firebase-app`. Specifically, open any terminal and provide the following command:

```
npx create-react-app storage-firebase-app
```

Initial Firebase Setup

Since our front-end site will also be hosted through Firebase, we will create the basic settings while this `create-react-app` command creates our React app. In this section, we will follow the same steps as in Chapter 1. I have created an app with name `storage-firebase-app` (Figure 4-2).

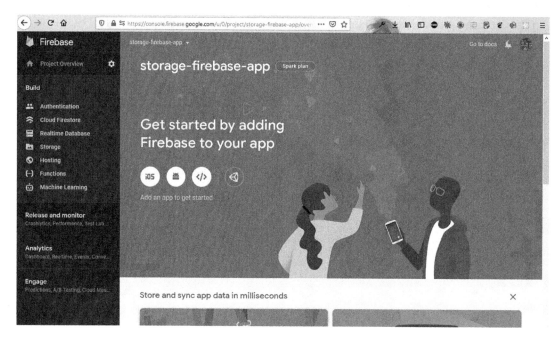

Figure 4-2. *Creating a storage app*

Now, click the **Settings** icon at the top-left corner of the screen. After that, click the **Project settings** button, as in Figure 4-3.

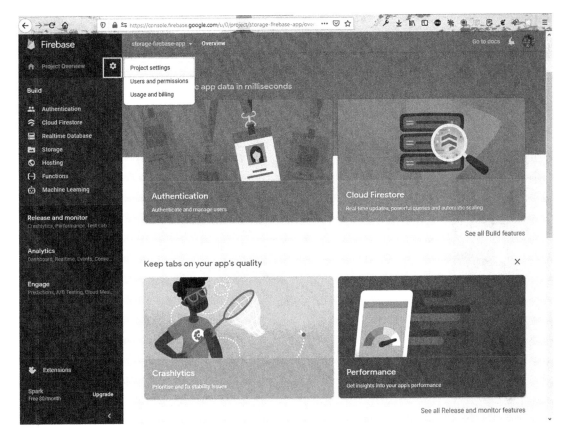

Figure 4-3. *Project settings*

Now, scroll down, click the **Config** radio button, and then copy all the code for the
`firebaseConfig` element, as shown in Figure 4-4.

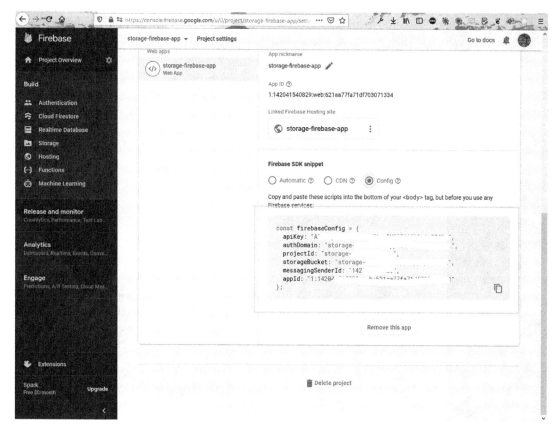

Figure 4-4. *Firebase configuration*

Basic React Setup

We will now complete our React setup. So, go back to the terminal and `cd` into the newly created `storage-firebase-app` directory.

After that, open the directory in VS Code and create a file named `firebase.js` inside the `src` folder. Paste the following content from the previous Firebase screen into that file:

```
const  xxxxxxConfig = {
    apiKey: "AIXXXXXXXXXXXXXXXXXXXXXXXXXXX",
    authDomain: "storage-XXXXXXXX.XXXXXXXXX.com",
    projectId: "storage- xxxxxx-app",
    storageBucket: "storage- xxxxxx-app.appspot.com",
    messagingSenderId: "14xxxxxxxx",
    appId: "1:142xxxxxxxxxxxxx:web:6xxxxxxxxxxx"
};
```

Inside the `storage-firebase-app` directory, start the React app with `npm start`. Next, we will delete some of the files because we don't need them. We are removing them because they show the React logo and other things, which need to be cleaned before starting the project. Figure 4-5 shows the files to be deleted.

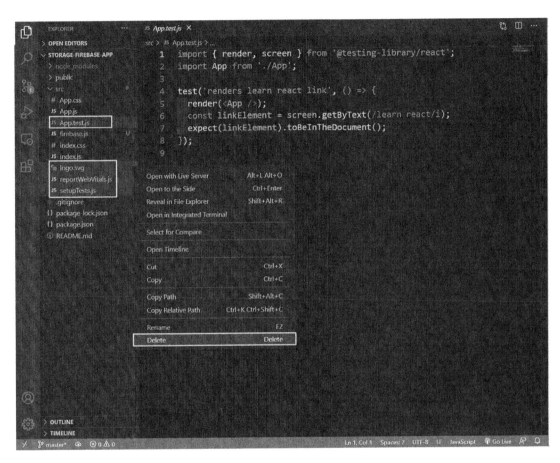

Figure 4-5. *Deleting files*

We will remove all the unnecessary boilerplate code, and our `index.js` file will look like this:

```
import React from 'react';
import ReactDOM from 'react-dom';
import './index.css';
import App from './App';
```

```
ReactDOM.render(
    <React.StrictMode>
        <App />
    </React.StrictMode>,
    document.getElementById('root')
);
```

The App.js file contains only the "Storage app React" text. We have also removed all the content from the App.css file.

```
import './App.css';

        function App() {
            return (
                <div className="app">
                <h1>Storage app React</h1>
                </div>
            );
        }
        export default App;
```

In the index.css file, update the CSS to use margin: 0 for all the content, as shown here:

```
*{
  margin: 0;
}
```

Creating a Header

Our React setup is done, and we will be working on the Header component first. So, create a folder called components inside the src folder. Create a Header.js file inside the components folder. We will import it first in the App.js file.

```
function App() {
  return (
    <div className="app">
```

```
        <Header />
      </div>
  );
}
export default App;
```

We will also be using Material UI for the icons. So, we need to do two `npm installs` per the documentation.

`npm i @material-ui/core @material-ui/icons`

Now, our `Header.js` file will mostly be static. It will mainly contain icons and logos.

Here, we have a `div` called `header`, containing three `div`s. The first one is `header__logo`, which contains an image and text. The next `div` is `header__searchContainer`, which contains a `SearchIcon`, an input box, and `ExpandMoreIcon`.

The third `div`, called `header__icons`, contains four icons: `HelpOutlineIcon`, `SettingsIcon`, `AppsIcon`, and `Avatar`.

```
import React from 'react'
import SearchIcon from '@material-ui/icons/Search'
import ExpandMoreIcon from '@material-ui/icons/ExpandMore'
import HelpOutlineIcon from '@material-ui/icons/HelpOutline'
import SettingsIcon from '@material-ui/icons/Settings'
import AppsIcon from '@material-ui/icons/Apps'
import { Avatar } from '@material-ui/core'
import './Header.css'

const Header = () => {
    return (
        <div className="header">
            <div className="header__logo">
                <img src="logo192.png" alt="logo" />
                <span>Storage</span>
            </div>
            <div className="header__searchContainer">
                <div className="header__searchBar">
                    <SearchIcon />
                    <input type="text" placeholder='Search in Storage' />
```

```
                    <ExpandMoreIcon />
                </div>
            </div>
            <div className="header__icons">
                <span>
                    <HelpOutlineIcon />
                    <SettingsIcon />
                </span>
                <AppsIcon />
                <Avatar className="header__iconsAvatar" />
            </div>
        </div>
    )
}
```

```
export default Header
```

Now, create a file called Header.css in the same folder and add the following content to it. Here, we are using a lot of flexboxes to style our header.

```
.header {
    display: flex;
    height: 60px;
    border-bottom: 1px solid rgb(219, 219, 219);
    width: 100vw;
}

.header>div {
    padding: 12px;
}

.header__logo {
    display: flex;
    justify-content: flex-start;
    align-items: center;
}
```

```
.header__logo>img {
    height: 100%;
    object-fit: contain;
}

.header__logo>span {
    color: gray;
    font-size: 20px;
    font-weight: 500;
    margin-left: 16px;
}

.header__searchContainer {
    flex: 1;
    display: flex;
    align-items: center;
    padding: 8px;
}

.header__searchBar {
    width: 45%;
    height: 120%;
    border-radius: 6px;
    background-color: rgb(237, 237, 237);
    display: flex;
    align-items: center;
    padding: 0 8px;
}

.MuiSvgIcon-root {
    color: rgb(82, 82, 82);
}

.header__searchBar>input {
    flex: 1;
    height: 60%;
    font-size: 16px;
    color: lightgray;
```

```
    background: none;
    border: none;
    margin-left: 12px;
}

.header__searchBar>input:focus {
    outline: none;
    color: black;
}

.header__icons {
    display: flex;
    align-items: center;
    margin-right: -30px;
}

.header__icons .MuiSvgIcon-root {
    font-size: 28px;
    color: rgb(82, 82, 82);
    margin: 4px;
}

.header__icons>span{
    margin-right: 20px;
}

.header__iconsAvatar{
    margin-right: 24px;
}
```

Now, our header is complete and looks like Figure 4-6 on localhost.

Figure 4-6. *Our header on localhost*

Creating the Sidebar

Now that our header component is complete, we will be creating the `Siderbar` component. For this, first import the `Siderbar` component into our `App.js` file. The code for this is shown in bold here:

```
import './App.css';
import Header from './components/Header';
import Sidebar from './components/Sidebar';

function App() {
  return (
    <div className="app">
    <Header />
    <Sidebar />
    </div>
  );
}
export default App;
```

Next, create a file called `Sidebar.js` in the components folder and add the following content in it. Here, we are calling two components: `FileComponent` and `SidebarItem`. In the `SidebarItem` components, we are also passing props, one of which is the icon.

```
import React from 'react';
import FileComponent from './FileComponent';
import SidebarItem from './SidebarItem';
import InsertDriveFileIcon from '@material-ui/icons/InsertDriveFile';
import ImportantDevicesIcon from '@material-ui/icons/ImportantDevices';
import PeopleAltIcon from '@material-ui/icons/PeopleAlt';
import QueryBuilderIcon from '@material-ui/icons/QueryBuilder';
import StarBorderIcon from '@material-ui/icons/StarBorder';
import DeleteOutlineIcon from '@material-ui/icons/DeleteOutline';
import StorageIcon from '@material-ui/icons/Storage';
import './Sidebar.css';
```

```
const Sidebar = () => {
    return (
        <div className="sidebar">
            <FileComponent />
            <div className="sidebar__itemsContainer">
                <SidebarItem arrow icon={(<InsertDriveFileIcon />)}
                label={'My Drive'} />
                <SidebarItem arrow icon={(<ImportantDevicesIcon />)}
                label={'Computers'} />
                <SidebarItem icon={(<PeopleAltIcon />)} label={'Shared with
                me'} />
                <SidebarItem icon={(<QueryBuilderIcon />)} label={'Recent'}
                />
                <SidebarItem icon={(<StarBorderIcon />)} label={'Starred'}
                />
                <SidebarItem icon={(<DeleteOutlineIcon />)} label={'Bin'}
                />
                <hr/>
                <SidebarItem icon={(<StorageIcon />)} label={'Storage'} />
            </div>
        </div>
    )
}

export default Sidebar
```

Now, create a FileComponent.js file in the same components folder. It contains AddIcon and New icons.

```
import React from 'react'
import AddIcon from '@material-ui/icons/Add'
import './FileComponent.css'

const FileComponent = () => {
    return (
        <div className="file">
            <div className="file__container">
```

```
            <AddIcon fontSize='large' />
            <p>New</p>
        </div>
    </div>
    )
}

export default FileComponent
```

Now, create a file called SidebarItem.js inside the components folder. It takes three props: arrow, icon, and label. We show ArrowRightIcon only if the arrow prop is passed.

```
import React from 'react'
import './SidebarItem.css'

import ArrowRightIcon from '@material-ui/icons/ArrowRight';

const SidebarItem = ({ arrow, icon, label }) => {
    return (
        <div className='sidebarItem'>
            <div className="sidebarItem__arrow">
                {arrow && (<ArrowRightIcon />)}
            </div>

            <div className='sidebarItem__main'>
                {icon}
                <p>{label}</p>
            </div>
        </div>

    )
}

export default SidebarItem
```

Figure 4-7 shows what the icons look like on localhost.

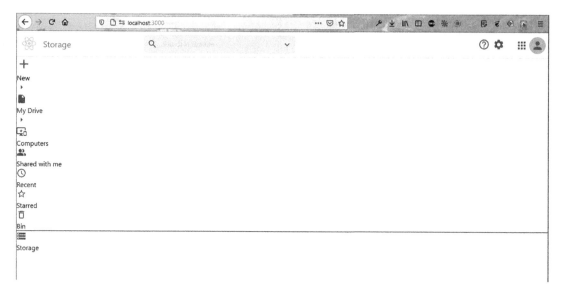

Figure 4-7. *Icons on localhost*

Now, it's time to fix our styles. So, add the following code in the `Sidebar.css` file:

```
.sidebar{
    width: 15%;
    height: 100vh;
    margin-right: 5px;
}

hr{
    background-color: rgb(197, 197, 197);
    height: 1px;
    border: none;
}
```

Next, in the `SidebarItem.css` file, add the following content:

```
.sidebarItem{
    display: flex;
    padding: 10px 0;
    border-radius: 0 100px 100px 0;
}
```

```
.sidebarItem:hover{
    background-color: rgba(0, 0, 0, 0.04);
}

.sidebarItem__arrow{
    width: 28px;
    margin-left: 12px;
}

.sidebarItem__main{
    display: flex;
}

.sidebarItem__main>p{
    margin-left: 12px;
}
```

In FileComponent.css, add the following content:

```
.file {
    display: flex;
    align-items: center;
    padding: 12px 0;
    padding-left: 20px;
}

.file__container {
    display: flex;
    justify-content: center;
    align-items: center;
    padding: 6px 32px 6px 8px;
    border-radius: 50px;
    box-shadow: 0 1px 2px 0 rgba(60, 64, 67, 0.302), 0 1px 3px 1px rgba(60, 64, 67, 0.149);
    cursor: pointer;
}

.file__container>p{
    margin-left: 14px;
}
```

The sidebar looks great, as shown in Figure 4-8.

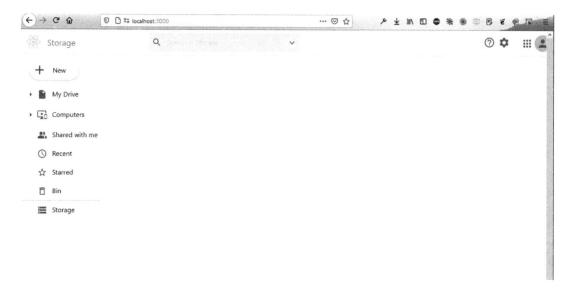

Figure 4-8. *Sidebar*

Uploading Files Using Firebase

We need to have some logic to upload the files, but for that we will need to have Firebase in our project first.

The first thing to do is install Firebase in our project by running the following command from the terminal:

```
npm i firebase
```

Next, we will update our `firebase.js` file to use the configuration to initialize the app. After that, we can use Firestore as the database. We are also using Google Authentication and storage in the project.

```
import firebase from 'firebase'

  const firebaseConfig = {
      ...
      ...
  };
```

```
const firebaseApp = firebase.initializeApp(firebaseConfig)

const auth = firebase.auth()
const provider = new firebase.auth.GoogleAuthProvider()
const storage = firebase.storage()
const db = firebaseApp.firestore()

export { auth, provider, db, storage }
```

Back in the FileComponent.js file, we will import the necessary modules. We are using Modal from Material UI here. The updated code is marked in bold here:

```
import React, { useState } from 'react'
import AddIcon from '@material-ui/icons/Add'
import './FileComponent.css'
import firebase from 'firebase'
import { storage, db } from '../firebase'
import { makeStyles } from '@material-ui/core/styles';
import Modal from '@material-ui/core/Modal';
function getModalStyle() {
    return {
    top: `50%`,
    left: `50%`,
    transform: `translate(-50%, -50%)`,
    };
}
const useStyles = makeStyles((theme) => ({
    paper: {
    position: 'absolute',
    width: 400,
    backgroundColor: theme.palette.background.paper,
    border: '2px solid #000',
    boxShadow: theme.shadows[5],
    padding: theme.spacing(2, 4, 3),
    },
}));
```

```
const FileComponent = () => {
    const classes = useStyles();
    const [modalStyle] = useState(getModalStyle);
    const [open, setOpen] = useState(false);
    const [file, setFile] = useState(null)
    const [uploading, setUploading] = useState(false)
    const handleOpen = () => { setOpen(true); };
    const handleClose = () => { setOpen(false); };
    return (
    <div className="file">
            <div className="file__container">
            <AddIcon fontSize='large' />
            <p>New</p>
            </div>
      </div>
    )
}

export default FileComponent
```

Now, inside the return block in FileComponent.js, we will show the Modal. The content of the Modal will be an input type file and a button. The updated code is marked in bold here:

```
...
...
    return (
        <div className="file">
                <div className="file__container" onClick={handleOpen}>
                <AddIcon fontSize='large' />
                <p>New</p>
                </div>
                <Modal
                open={open}
                onClose={handleClose}
                aria-labelledby="simple-modal-title"
```

```
            aria-describedby="simple-modal-description"
            >
            <div style={modalStyle} className={classes.paper}>
            <p>Select files you want to upload!</p>
            {
                uploading ? (
                <p>Uploading...</p>
                ) : (
                <>
                <input type="file" onChange={handleChange} />
                <button onClick=
                {handleUpload}>Upload</button>
                </>
                )
            }
            </div>
            </Modal>
        </div>
        )
...
...
```

Next, we will create the handleChange and handleUpload functions in the FileComponent.js file. In the handleChange function, we are setting the file to setFile(), and inside the handleUpload function, we are taking the uploaded file and saving its various elements, such as its caption, in fileUrl. These will be shown later in our app. The updated code is marked in bold here:

```
...
...
const FileComponent = () => {
  ...
  ...

    const handleChange = (e) => {
    if (e.target.files[0]) {
```

```
    setFile(e.target.files[0])
    }
}

const handleUpload = () => {
setUploading(true)
storage.ref(`files/${file.name}`).put(file).then(snapshot => {
console.log(snapshot)
storage.ref('files').child(file.name).getDownloadURL().then(url => {
                db.collection('myFiles').add({
                timestamp: firebase.firestore.FieldValue.
                serverTimestamp(),
                caption: file.name,
                fileUrl: url,
                size: snapshot._delegate.bytesTransferred,
                })
                setUploading(false)
                setOpen(false)
                setFile(null)
    })

storage.ref('files').child(file.name).getMetadata().then(meta => {
console.log(meta.size)
    })

    })
    }

    return (
    ...
    ...
    )
}

export default FileComponent
```

For our code to work, we need to set up storage in Firebase. So, from the Firebase console, click **Storage** and then **Get Started**. Now, the pop-up shown in Figure 4-9 will display, where you need to click the **Next** button.

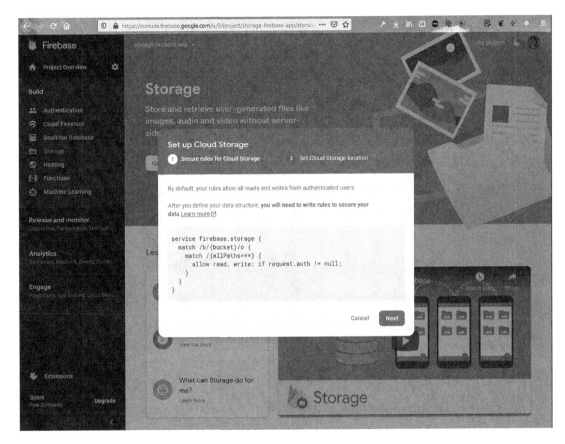

Figure 4-9. *Getting started*

On the next screen, just click the **Done** button, as shown in Figure 4-10.

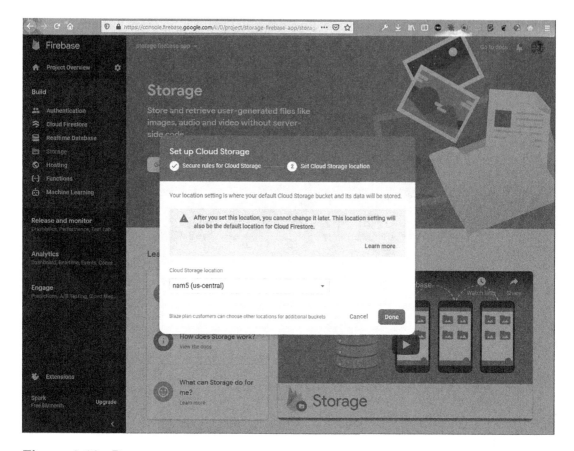

Figure 4-10. *Done*

Firebase requires authentication to upload files. Since we have not set up authentication yet, we need to change the rules, as shown in Figure 4-11.

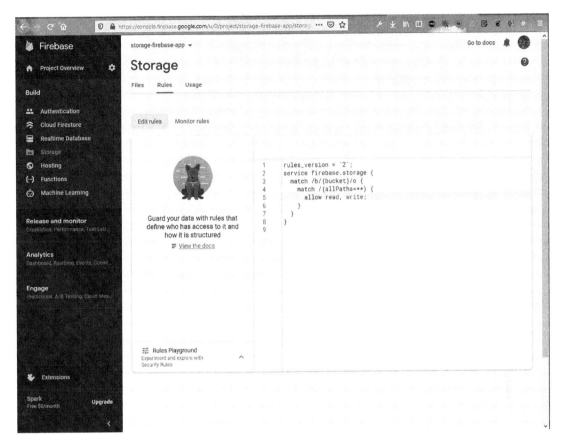

Figure 4-11. *Rules*

Now, back on localhost, click the **New** button, which will display a pop-up. In the pop-up, you can upload any file, as shown in Figure 4-12.

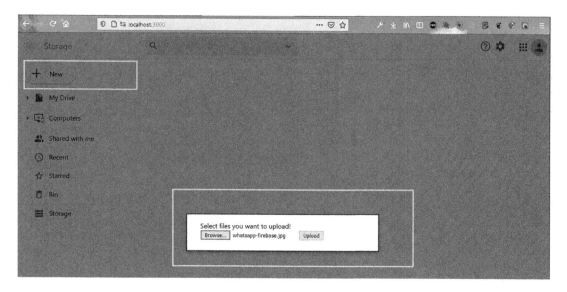

Figure 4-12. *Pop-up to upload a file*

Clicking the **Upload** button after selecting a file will upload the file to Firebase, as shown in Figure 4-13.

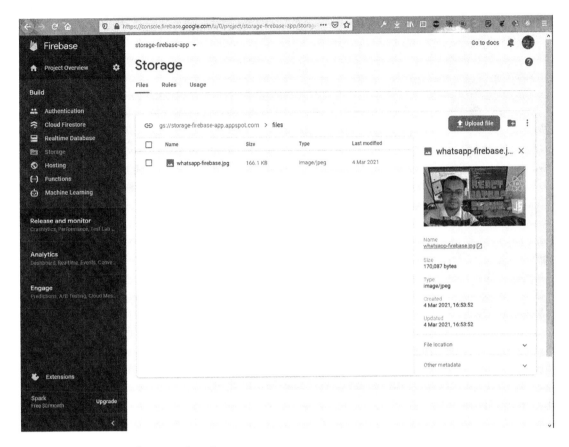

Figure 4-13. *Firebase upload*

Displaying Files with the FileViewer Component

We have the logic to upload the files, but now we want to display the files in our project.

We also need to enable Firestore first. For that, go back to the Firebase console and click **Cloud Firestore** and then the **Create database** button, as shown in Figure 4-14.

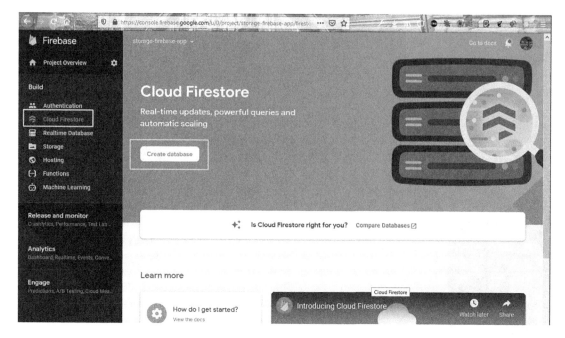

Figure 4-14. *Creating a database*

On the next screen, select **Start in test mode** and then click the **Next** button, as shown in Figure 4-15.

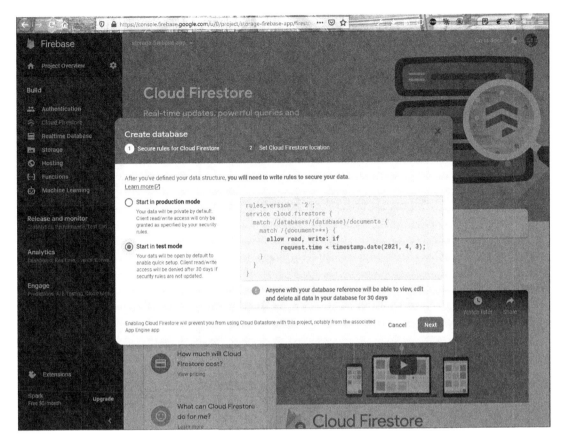

Figure 4-15. *Test mode*

After that, on the next screen, click the **Enable** button, as shown in Figure 4-16.

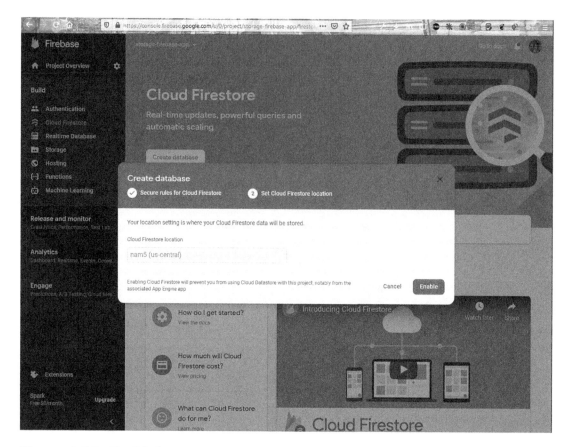

Figure 4-16. *Enable button*

Now, create a file called `FilesViewer.js` and add the following content in it. Here, we are getting all the file details from Firebase by calling `FilesViewer.js` inside the `useEffect` hook. After getting the data, we are mapping through it and passing it to the `FileItem` component, which we will create next.

```
import React, { useEffect, useState } from 'react'
import './FilesViewer.css'
import { db } from '../firebase'
import FileItem from './FileItem'

const FilesViewer = () => {
    const [files, setFiles] = useState()
```

```
useEffect(() => {
        db.collection('myFiles').onSnapshot(snapshot => {
            setFiles(snapshot.docs.map(doc => ({
                id: doc.id,
                item: doc.data()
            })))
        })
    }, [])

    return (
        <div className='fileViewer'>
            <div className="fileViewer__row">
            </div>
            <div className="fileViewer__titles">
                <div className="fileViewer__titles--left">
                    <p>Name</p>
                </div>
                <div className="fileViewer__titles--right">
                    <p>Last modified</p>
                    <p>File size</p>
                </div>
            </div>
            {
                files.map(({ id, item }) => (
                    <FileItem id={id} caption={item.caption}
                    timestamp={item.timestamp} fileUrl={item.fileUrl}
                    size={item.size} />
                ))
            }
        </div>
    )
}

export default FilesViewer
```

Next, create a file named FileItem.js and add the following content in it. Here, we are just displaying the data. But one of the main things is the readableFileSizeStr function. Through this function we are showing the correct numbers.

```
import React from 'react'
import './FileItem.css'

import InsertDriveFileIcon from '@material-ui/icons/InsertDriveFile';

const monthNames = ["Jan", "Feb", "Mar", "Apr", "May", "Jun", "Jul", "Aug",
"Sep", "Oct", "Nov", "Dec"];

const FileItem = ({ id, caption, timestamp, fileUrl, size }) => {
    const fileDate = `${timestamp?.toDate().getDate()}
    ${monthNames[timestamp?.toDate().getMonth() + 1]} ${timestamp?.
    toDate().getFullYear()}`

const readableFileSizeStr = (fileSizeInBytes) => {
        let i = -1;
        const byteUnits = [' kB', ' MB', ' GB', ' TB', 'PB', 'EB', 'ZB', 'YB'];
        do {
            fileSizeInBytes = fileSizeInBytes / 1024;
            i++;
        } while (fileSizeInBytes > 1024);
        return Math.max(fileSizeInBytes, 0.1).toFixed(1) + byteUnits[i];
    };

return (
        <div className='fileItem'>
            <a href={fileUrl} target="_blank" rel="noreferrer" download>
                <div className="fileItem--left">
                    <InsertDriveFileIcon />
                    <p>{caption}</p>
                </div>
                <div className="fileItem--right">
                    <p>{fileDate}</p>
                    <p>{readableFileSizeStr(size)}</p>
```

```
            </div>
         </a>
      </div>
   )
}
```

```
export default FileItem
```

Now, back in `App.js` we have included the `FilesViewer` component and also added a div called `app__main` to contain it and the `Sidebar` component. The updated code for this is marked in bold:

```
import './App.css';
import Header from './components/Header';
import Sidebar from './components/Sidebar';
import FilesViewer from './components/FilesViewer';

function App() {
  return (
     <div className="app">
     <Header />
     <div className="app__main">
           <Sidebar />
           <FilesViewer />
     </div>
     </div>
  );
}
export default App;
```

Next, in `App.css`, add the following styles:

```
.app__main{
    display: flex;
}
```

Now, back on localhost, we have to upload another file; then we will see the file details, as shown in Figure 4-17.

Figure 4-17. *File details*

Now, we will add styles in these components. First add the styles in the FileItem.
css file.

```
.fileItem{
    height: 55px;
    border-bottom: 1px solid rgb(219, 219, 219);
    border-top: 1px solid rgb(219, 219, 219);
    width: 100%;
}

.fileItem>a{
    height: 100%;
    display: flex;
    text-decoration: none;
    color: rgb(85, 78, 78);
}

.fileItem>a>div{
    display: flex;
align-items: center;
}
```

```css
.fileItem>a>div>*{
    margin: 10px;
}

.fileItem--left{
    flex: 1;
}
```

Next, add the styles in the FilesViewer.css file.

```css
.fileViewer{
width: 100%;
}

.fileViewer__row{
    height: 250px;
    display: flex;
    align-items: center;
}

.fileViewer__titles{
    display: flex;
    margin-bottom: 5px;
    color: rgb(85, 78, 78);
}

.fileViewer__titles>div>*{
    margin: 5px;
}

    .fileViewer__titles--left{
        flex: 1;
}

.fileViewer__titles--right{
    display: flex;
}
```

Now, our file is looking great on localhost, as shown in Figure 4-18.

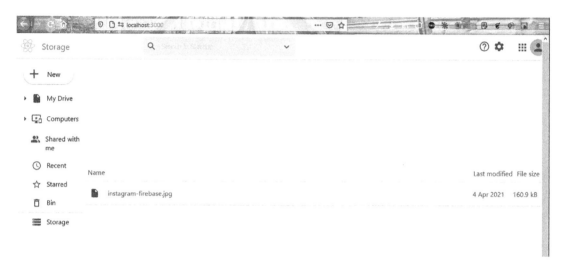

Figure 4-18.   *The layout*

Creating the FileCard Component

We now create a `FileCard` component to show nice icons for the files in our project.

Create a file named `FileCard.js` and put the following content in it. Here, we are just showing a big icon and the name of the file, passed from the parent component.

```
import React from 'react'
import './FileCard.css'

import InsertDriveFileIcon from '@material-ui/icons/InsertDriveFile';

const FileCard = ({ name }) => {
    return (
        <div className='fileCard'>
            <div className="fileCard--top">
                <InsertDriveFileIcon style={{ fontSize: 130 }} />
            </div>
            <div className="fileCard--bottom">
                <p>{name}</p>
            </div>
```

```
        </div>
    )
}

export default FileCard
```

Next, in FileCard.css, put the following styles:

```css
.fileCard {
    height: 190px;
    width: 240px;
    border-radius: 10px;
    border: 1px solid rgb(219, 219, 219);
    margin: 5px;
}

.fileCard--top {
    height: 70%;
    border-bottom: 1px solid rgb(219, 219, 219);
    display: flex;
    justify-content: center;
    align-items: center;
}

.fileCard--bottom {
    display: flex;
    align-items: center;
    justify-content: center;
    width: 100%;
    height: 30%;
}

.fileCard--bottom>p {
    width: 90%;
    overflow: hidden;
    white-space: nowrap;
}
```

Now, we need to import the FileCard component in the FilesViewer.js file. Here, we are mapping through all the files but selecting only five and sending the name value to the FileCard component. The updated code is marked as bold here:

```
...
import FileCard from './FileCard'

const FilesViewer = () => {
    ...
    ...

      return (
      <div className='fileViewer'>
         <div className="fileViewer__row">
         {
         files.slice(0, 5).map(({ id, item }) => (
         <FileCard key={id} name={item.caption} />
         ))

         }
         </div>
         ...
         ...
      </div>
      )
}

export default FilesViewer
```

Now, we can see a big icon on localhost, as shown in Figure 4-19.

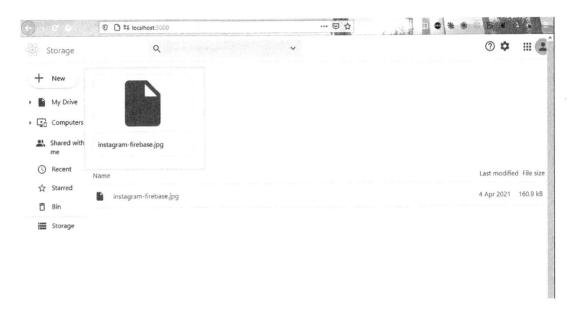

Figure 4-19. *Big icon*

Creating the SideIcons Component

We now create a SideIcons component to show some nice icons on the side. Create a file called SideIcons.js and put the following content in it:

```
import React from 'react'
import './SideIcons.css'
import AddIcon from '@material-ui/icons/Add'

const SideIcons = () => {
    return (
        <div className='sideIcons'>
            <div className="sideIcons__top">
                <img src="https://cdn4.iconfinder.com/data/icons/logos-
                brands-in-colors/48/google-calendar-512.png"
                alt="Calendar" />
                <img src="https://assets.materialup.com/uploads/64f5506e-
                2577-4d19-9425-11a1e1fa31a8/0x0ss-85.jpg" alt="Keep" />
```

```
                    <img src="https://www.androidpolice.com/wp-content/
                    uploads/2018/03/nexus2cee_new-tasks-icon.png" alt="Tasks"
                    />
                </div>
                <hr />
                <div className="sideIcons__plusIcon">
                    <AddIcon />
                </div>
            </div>
        )
}

export default SideIcons
```

Next, in SideIcons.css, put the following styles:

```
.sideIcons{
    width: 50px;
    display: flex;
    flex-direction: column;
    align-items: center;
    border-left: 1px solid rgb(219, 219, 219);
}

.sideIcons__top{
    width: 100%;
    display: flex;
    flex-direction: column;
    align-items: center;
}

.sideIcons__top>img{
    object-fit: contain;
    width: 30px;
    margin: 10px 0;
}
```

```
.sideIcons>hr{
    margin: 12px 0;
    width: 90%;
}

.sideIcons__plusIcon{
    display: flex;
    align-items: center;
}
```

Now, import the code in the App.js file. The updated code for this is marked in bold here:

```
...
import SideIcons from './components/SideIcons';

function App() {
  return (
      <div className="app">
      <Header />
      <div className="app__main">
      <Sidebar />
      <FilesViewer />
      <SideIcons />
      </div>
      </div>
  );
}
export default App;
```

Now, we can see these nice icons in the right sidebar, as in Figure 4-20.

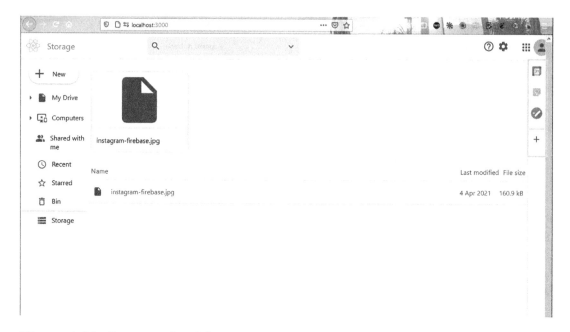

Figure 4-20. *Icons on the right*

Adding Google Authentication

Now, our app is almost complete, but we still need to add Google Authentication to it. So, go to the Firebase console and click the **Authentication** tab and then the **Get started** button, as shown in Figure 4-21.

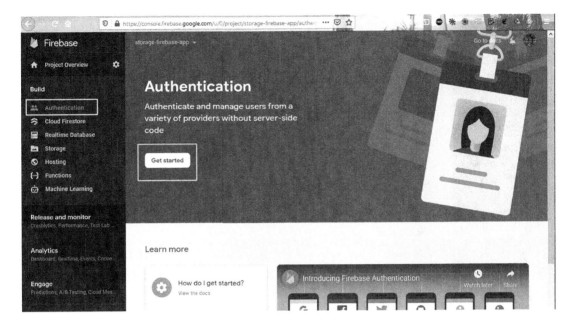

Figure 4-21. *Getting started with authentication*

On the next screen, click the **Edit configuration** icon beside Google, as shown in Figure 4-22.

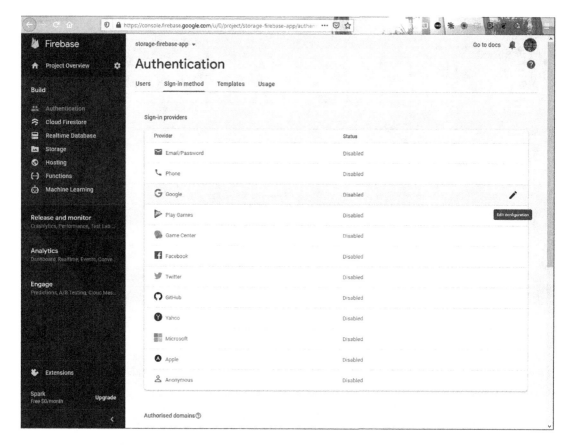

Figure 4-22. *Clicking Google*

In the pop-up message, click the **Enable** button, and after that enter your Gmail ID and click the **Save** button, as shown in Figure 4-23.

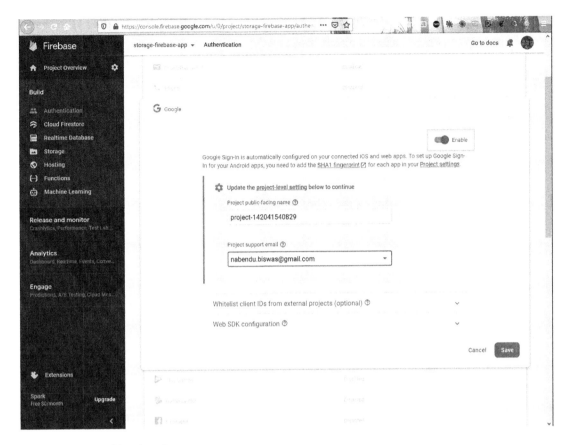

Figure 4-23. *Signing in*

Next in the App.js file, we just need to import auth and provider from our local Firebase file. After that, we use the method called signInWithPopup() to enable authentication.

After that, inside the return block, we are using a ternary operator to show all the components, if we have a user. We show a login div if no user is found. The updated code for this is marked in bold here:

```
import { auth, provider } from "./firebase";
import { useState } from 'react';

function App() {
  const [user, setUser] = useState(null)
  const handleLogin = () => {
    if (!user) {
```

```
        auth.signInWithPopup(provider).then(result => setUser(result.user))
         .catch(error => alert(error.message));
      }
    }

  return (
        <div className="app">
        {user ? (
        <>
        <Header userPhoto={user?.photoURL}/>
        <div className="app__main">
        <Sidebar />
        <FilesViewer />
        <SideIcons />
        </div>
        </>
        ) : (
        <div className='app__login'>
        <img src="logo512.png" alt="Storage" />
        <button onClick={handleLogin}>Log in to Storage</button>
        </div>
        )}
        </div>
    );
}
export default App;
```

Now, in the App.css file, add these additional styles:

```
.app__login {
    width: 100vw;
    height: 100vh;
    display: grid;
    place-items: center;
}

.app__login>button{
    border: none;
```

```
    font-size: 24px;
    background-color: rgb(67, 130, 244);
    color: white;
    padding: 10px 20px;
    border-radius: 6px;
    transition: all 0.2s;
}

.app__login>button:hover{
    cursor: pointer;
    background-color: rgb(49, 94, 179);
    transform: scale(1.1);
}
```

Since we are passing the userPhoto props to the Header component, we will use it in the Header.js file.The updated code for this is marked in bold here:

```
...
const Header = ({ userPhoto }) => {
return (
        <div className="header">
            ...
            ...
            <div className="header__icons">
            <span>
            <HelpOutlineIcon />
            <SettingsIcon />
            </span>
            <AppsIcon />
            <Avatar className="header__iconsAvatar"
            src={userPhoto} />
            </div>
        </div>
        )
}

export default Header
```

Now, when we go to localhost and click **Log in to Storage**, we will see the Google Authentication pop-up, as shown in Figure 4-24.

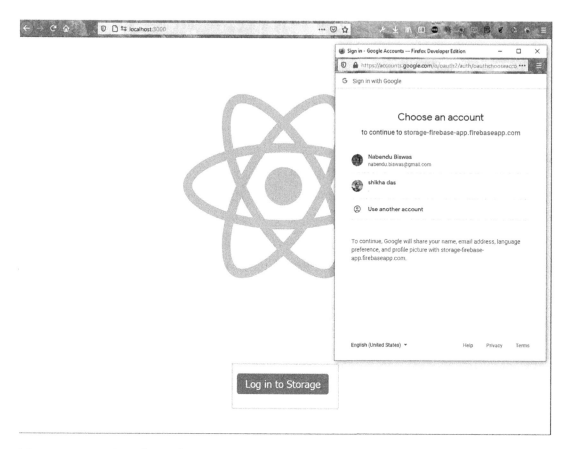

Figure 4-24. *Google Authentication pop-up*

When we click the Gmail ID, we will be taken to our app. Here, we can see the logged-in user image at the top-right corner, as shown in Figure 4-25.

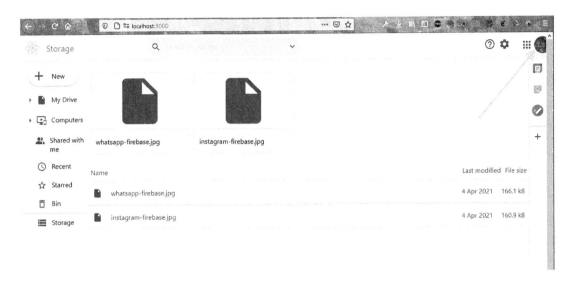

Figure 4-25. Logged-in user

Deploying and Hosting Through Firebase

Now we can deploy our app in Firebase by following the same steps as described earlier. The deployment was successful and working properly, as shown in Figure 4-26.

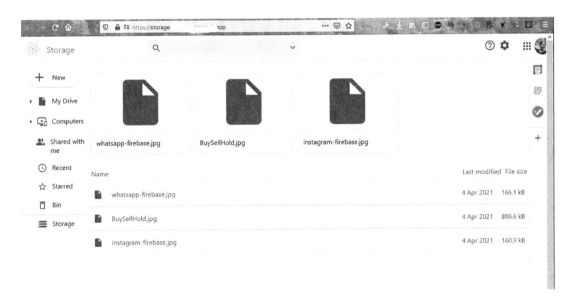

Figure 4-26. Storage app

Summary

In this chapter, you learned how to make a storage app, where you can log in through Google Authentication and can upload files. We created the web app with React and stored the data in Firebase storage. You also learned how to do the hosting in Firebase.

CHAPTER 5

Building a Career-Related Social Media App with React and Firebase

Welcome to a new ReactJS project, which is going to be a career-related social media app built in ReactJS. Also, we will use Redux and a lot of other wonderful technologies to create this app.

The hosting and the database will be in Firebase. We will also be using Material UI for the icons in the project.

Figure 5-1 shows the complete app.

© Nabendu Biswas 2022
N. Biswas, *Beginning React and Firebase*, https://doi.org/10.1007/978-1-4842-7812-3_5

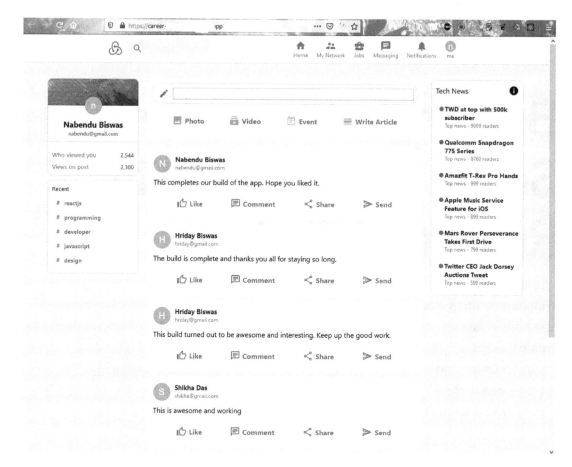

Figure 5-1. *Completed app*

Getting Started

Use the `create-react-app` command to create a new app called `career-firebase-app`. Specifically, open any terminal and enter the following command. Notice that we are using `template redux` to include Redux in our project.

```
npx create-react-app career-firebase-app --template redux
```

Initial Firebase Setup

Since our front-end site will also be hosted through Firebase, we will create the basic settings while this `create-react-app` command creates our React app. We will follow the same steps as in Chapter 1. I have created an app with the name `career-firebase-app` (Figure 5-2).

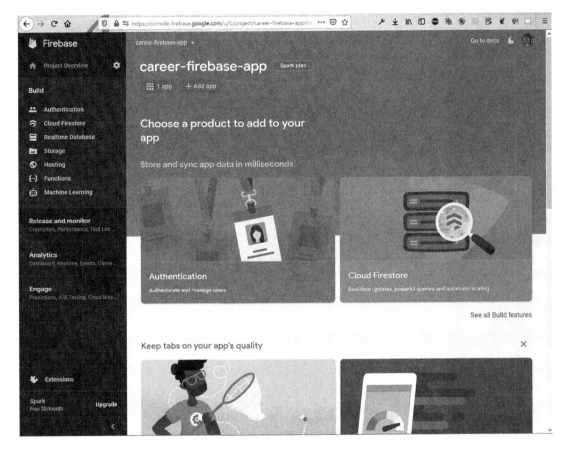

Figure 5-2. *career-firebase-app*

We will also enable Cloud Firestore like we did in the previous chapter. Lastly, copy all the code for firebaseConfig, as shown in Figure 5-3. (You can find the steps for doing this in the previous chapter.)

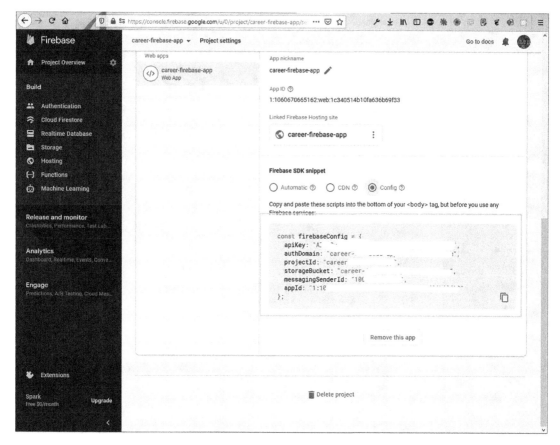

Figure 5-3. *Config*

Basic React Setup

Our React setup will have completed by this time. So, go back to the terminal and cd into the newly created `career-firebase-app` directory.

After that, open the directory in VS Code and create a file called `firebase.js` inside the `src` folder and paste the content from the previous Firebase screen into it.

```
const  xxxxxxConfig = {
    apiKey: "AXXXXXXXXXXXXXXXXXXXXXXXXX",
    authDomain: "career- xxxxxx-app. xxxxxxapp.com",
    projectId: "career- xxxxxx-app",
    storageBucket: "career- xxxxxx-app.appspot.com",
```

```
    messagingSenderId: "106xxxxxxxxxxxxxx",
    appId: "1:10xxxxxxxxxxx:web:1xxxxxxxxxxxxxx"
};
```

Next, we will do the cleanup process, which is similar to what we did in the previous chapter. First we'll delete the unnecessary files and change index.js.

```
import React from 'react';
import ReactDOM from 'react-dom';
import './index.css';
import App from './App';
import store from './app/store';
import { Provider } from 'react-redux';

ReactDOM.render(
  <React.StrictMode>
    <Provider store={store}>
      <App />
    </Provider>
  </React.StrictMode>,
  document.getElementById('root')
);
```

Then we'll change App.js, as shown here:

```
import React from 'react';
import './App.css';

function App() {
  return (
    <div className="app">
      <h1>Career Firebase App</h1>
    </div>
  );
}

export default App;
```

Now both files contain the bare minimum. Also, remove everything from App.css and make the margins zero in index.css. Our localhost will look like Figure 5-4 after the process.

Figure 5-4. *Initial app*

Creating the Header

Our React setup is done, and we will be working on the Header component first. So, create a folder named components inside the src folder. Create the Header.js and Header.css files inside the components folder. But we will import Header component first in the App.js file.

```
import React from 'react';
import './App.css';
import Header from './components/Header';

function App() {
  return (
    <div className="app">
        <Header />
    </div>
  );
}

export default App;
```

We will be using Material UI for the icons. So, we need to do two npm installs per the documentation. We will install core and icons through the integrated terminal.

```
npm i @material-ui/core @material-ui/icons
```

Now, our Header.js files will be static mostly. File will contain mainly icons and logos.

Here, we have a div called header, containing two divs. The first one is header__ left, which contains an image and another div containing Search as input. The next div is header__right, which contains a call to another component, called HeaderOption.

```
import { Search, Home, SupervisorAccount, BusinessCenter, Chat,
Notifications } from '@material-ui/icons'
import React from 'react'
import './Header.css'
import HeaderOption from './HeaderOption'

const Header = () => {
    return (
        <div className="header">
            <div className="header__left">
                <img src="logo192.png" alt="logo"/>
                <div className="header__search">
                    <Search />
                    <input type="text"/>
                </div>
            </div>
            <div className="header__right">
                <HeaderOption Icon={Home} title="Home" />
                <HeaderOption Icon={SupervisorAccount} title=
                "My Network" />
                <HeaderOption Icon={BusinessCenter} title="Jobs" />
                <HeaderOption Icon={Chat} title="Messaging" />
                <HeaderOption Icon={Notifications} title="Notifications" />
                <HeaderOption avatar="https://pbs.twimg.com/profile_
                images/1020939891457241088/fcbu814K_400x400.jpg" title="me"
                />
            </div>
        </div>
    )
}

export default Header
```

Now, create a file called Header.css in the same folder and add the following content in it. Here, we are using a lot of flexboxes to style our header.

```css
.header{
    position: sticky;
    top: 0;
    display: flex;
    background-color: white;
    justify-content: space-evenly;
    border-bottom: 0.1px solid lightgray;
    padding: 10px 0;
    width: 100%;
    z-index: 999;
}

.header__left{
    display: flex;
}

.header__left > img{
    object-fit: contain;
    height: 40px;
    margin-right: 10px;
}

.header__search{
    padding: 10px;
    display: flex;
    align-items: center;
    border-radius: 5px;
    height: 22px;
    color:gray;
    background-color: #eef3f8;
}

.header__search > input{
    outline: none;
    border: none;
```

```
    background: none;
}

.header__right{
    display: flex;
}
```

Next, create the HeaderOption.js file, which will take an avatar, icon, title, and props, as shown here:

```
import { Avatar } from '@material-ui/core'
import React from 'react'
import './HeaderOption.css'

const HeaderOption = ({ avatar, Icon, title }) => {
    return (
        <div className="headerOption">
            {Icon && <Icon className="headerOption__icon" />}
            {avatar && <Avatar className="headerOption__icon" src={avatar}
            />}
            <h3 className="headerOption__title">{title}</h3>
        </div>
    )
}

export default HeaderOption
```

Now, create the style for this in the HeaderOption.css file.

```
.headerOption{
    display: flex;
    flex-direction: column;
    align-items: center;
    margin-right: 20px;
    color:gray;
    cursor: pointer;
}
```

```css
.headerOption:hover{
    color: black;
}

.headerOption__title{
    font-size: 12px;
    font-weight: 400;
}

.headerOption__icon{
    object-fit: contain;
    height: 25px !important;
    width: 25px !important;
}
```

Now, on localhost, we can see the nice header shown in Figure 5-5.

Figure 5-5. *Our header*

Creating the Sidebar

We will be working on the Sidebar component now. So, create the Sidebar.js and Sidebar.css files inside the folder components. But we will import Sidebar first in the App.js file. The updated code is shown in bold, as shown here:

```jsx
import Sidebar from './components/Sidebar';

function App() {
  return (
      <div className="app">
      <Header />
      <div className="app__body">
            <Sidebar />
      </div>
```

```
        </div>
    );
}
export default App;
```

Next, we will also add styles for app and app__body in the App.css file.

```
.app{
    background-color: #f3f2ef;
    display: flex;
    flex-direction: column;
    align-items: center;
}

.app__body{
    display: flex;
}
```

Next put the following content in the file Sidebar.js. Here, the primary div of the sidebar contains three divs: sidebar__top, sidebar__stats, and sidebar__bottom.

- The sidebar__top contains an image, avatar, name, and email. For the image, I have put one image in the public folder so that we can use it directly.

- The sidebar__stats contains two divs called sidebar__stat, each of which contains a text and a number paragraph.

- The sidebar__bottom contains only a p tag with the "Recent" word as of now.

```
import { Avatar } from '@material-ui/core'
import React from 'react'
import './Sidebar.css'

const Sidebar = () => {
    return (
        <div className="sidebar">
            <div className="sidebar__top">
```

```
                <img src="background.jpg" alt="Background" />
                <Avatar className="sidebar__avatar" />
                <h2>Nabendu Biswas</h2>
                <h4>nabendu.biswas@gmail.com</h4>
            </div>
            <div className="sidebar__stats">
                <div className="sidebar__stat">
                    <p>Who viewed you</p>
                    <p className="sidebar__statNumber">2,544</p>
                </div>
                <div className="sidebar__stat">
                    <p>Views on post</p>
                    <p className="sidebar__statNumber">2,300</p>
                </div>
            </div>
            <div className="sidebar__bottom">
                <p>Recent</p>
            </div>
        </div>
    )
}

export default Sidebar
```

Now, put the following styles in the Sidebar.css file:

```
.sidebar{
    position: sticky;
    top: 80px;
    flex: 0.2;
    border-radius: 10px;
    text-align: center;
    height: fit-content;
}

.sidebar__avatar{
    margin-bottom: 10px;
}
```

```css
.sidebar__top{
    display: flex;
    flex-direction: column;
    align-items: center;
    border: 1px solid lightgray;
    border-bottom: 0;
    border-top-left-radius: 10px;
    border-top-right-radius: 10px;
    background-color: white;
    padding-bottom: 10px;
}

.sidebar__top > img{
    margin-bottom: -20px;
    width: 100%;
    height: 60px;
    border-top-left-radius: 10px;
    border-top-right-radius: 10px;
    object-fit: cover;
}

.sidebar__top > h4{
    color: gray;
    font-size: 12px;
}

.sidebar__top > h2{
    font-size: 18px;
}

.sidebar__stats{
    padding: 10px;
    margin-bottom: 10px;
    border: 1px solid lightgray;
    background-color: white;
    border-bottom-left-radius: 10px;
    border-bottom-right-radius: 10px;
}
```

```
.sidebar__stat{
    margin-top: 10px;
    display: flex;
    justify-content: space-between;
}

.sidebar__stat > p{
    color: gray;
    font-size: 13px;
    font-weight: 600;
}

.sidebar__statNumber{
    font-weight: bold;
    color: #0a66c2 !important;
}

.sidebar__bottom{
    text-align: left;
    padding: 10px;
    border: 1px solid lightgray;
    background-color: white;
    border-radius: 10px;
    margin-top: 10px;
}
```

Now, our sidebar looks like Figure 5-6 on localhost.

Figure 5-6. *Our sidebar*

Now, we will put all items in sidebar__bottom in the Sidebar.js file. Here, we have created the function recentItem and are passing different props to it. The updated code for this is shown in bold here:

```
const Sidebar = () => {
    const recentItem = (topic) => (
    <div className="sidebar__recentItem">
        <span className="sidebar__hash">#</span>
        <p>{topic}</p>
    </div>
    )

    return (
    <div className="sidebar">
            ...
            ...
            <div className="sidebar__bottom">
            <p>Recent</p>
            {recentItem("reactjs")}
            {recentItem("programming")}
            {recentItem("developer")}
            {recentItem("javascript")}
            {recentItem("design")}
            </div>
        </div>
        )
}

export default Sidebar
```

Next, we will put additional styles in the Sidebar.css file, as shown here:

```
.sidebar__bottom > p{
    font-size: 13px;
    padding-bottom: 10px;
}
```

```
.sidebar__recentItem{
    display: flex;
    font-size: 13px;
    color: gray;
    font-weight: bolder;
    cursor: pointer;
    margin-bottom: 5px;
    padding: 5px;
}

.sidebar__recentItem:hover{
    background-color: whitesmoke;
    border-radius: 10px;
    cursor: pointer;
    color: black;
}

.sidebar__hash{
    margin-right: 10px;
    margin-left: 5px;
}
```

Now, our localhost will look like Figure 5-7 with the Recent box.

Figure 5-7. *Recent box*

Creating the Feed Component

We will be working on the Feed component now. So, inside the folder `components`, create files called `Feed.js` and `Feed.css` in the folder `components`. But we will import `Feed` component first in the `App.js` file. The updated code for this is shown in bold here:

```
import Feed from './components/Feed';

function App() {
  return (
    <div className="app">
    <Header />
    <div className="app__body">
    <Sidebar />
    <Feed />
    </div>
    </div>
  );
}

export default App;
```

Next, put the following content in the file `Feed.js`. Here, the primary `div` of `feed` contains a `div` called `feed__inputContainer`, which contains two `divs`: `feed__input` and `feed__inputOptions`.

- The `feed__input` contains a create icon and a form. The form contains an input and a button.

- The `feed__inputOptions` is calling a component `InputOption` with `Icon`, `title`, and `color` props. The `Icon` prop is actually a Material UI icon.

```
import { CalendarViewDay, Create, EventNote, Image, Subscriptions } from
'@material-ui/icons'
import React from 'react'
import './Feed.css'
import InputOption from './InputOption'
```

```
const Feed = () => {
    return (
        <div className="feed">
            <div className="feed__inputContainer">
                <div className="feed__input">
                    <Create />
                    <form>
                        <input type="text"/>
                        <button type="submit">Send</button>
                    </form>
                </div>
                <div className="feed__inputOptions">
                    <InputOption Icon={Image} title="Photo"
                    color="#70B5F9" />
                    <InputOption Icon={Subscriptions} title="Video"
                    color="#E7A33E" />
                    <InputOption Icon={EventNote} title="Event"
                    color="#C0CBCD" />
                    <InputOption Icon={CalendarViewDay} title="Write
                    Article" color="#7FC15E" />
                </div>
            </div>
        </div>
    )
}

export default Feed
```

Now, put the following styles in the Feed.css file:

```
.feed{
    flex: 0.6;
    margin: 0 20px;
}

.feed__inputContainer{
    background-color: white;
    padding: 10px;
```

```css
    padding-bottom: 20px;
    border-radius: 10px;
    margin-bottom: 20px;
}

.feed__input{
    border: 1px solid lightgray;
    border-radius: 30px;
    display: flex;
    padding: 10px;
    color: gray;
    padding-left: 15px;
}

.feed__input > form{
    display: flex;
    width: 100%;
}

.feed__input > form > input{
    border: none;
    flex: 1;
    margin-left: 10px;
    outline-width: 0;
    font-weight: 600;
}

.feed__input > form > button{
    display: none;
}

.feed__inputOptions{
    display: flex;
    justify-content: space-evenly;
}
```

Now, create a file called InputOption.js and put the following content in it. The component is mainly used to show different icons with props passed to it.

```
import React from 'react'
import './InputOption.css'

const InputOption = ({ Icon, title, color }) => {
    return (
        <div className="inputOption">
            <Icon style={{ color }} />
            <h4>{title}</h4>
        </div>
    )
}

export default InputOption
```

Now, we will create the styles for this in the InputOption.css file.

```
.inputOption{
    display: flex;
    align-items: center;
    margin-top: 15px;
    color: gray;
    padding: 10px;
    cursor: pointer;
}

.inputOption:hover{
    background-color: whitesmoke;
    border-radius: 10px;
}

.inputOption > h4{
    margin-left: 5px;
}
```

Our Feed component is complete and looks like Figure 5-8 on localhost.

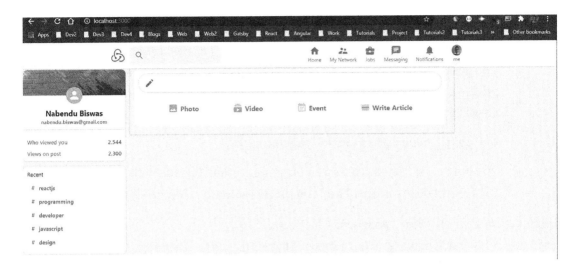

Figure 5-8. *Add Post section*

Building the Post Section

We will be working on the Post section now. So, inside the folder components, create files called Post.js and Post.css. But we will import Post component first into the Feed.js file. Also, notice that we are passing three props to it: name, description, and message. The updated code is shown in bold here:

```
import Post from './Post'

const Feed = () => {
      return (
      <div className="feed">
      <div className="feed__inputContainer">
            ...
            ...
      </div>
      <Post name="Nabendu Biswas" description="This is a test"
      message="This is awesome thing to do" />
      </div>
      )
}

export default Feed
```

Next put the following content in the file Post.js. Here, the primary div of post contains three divs: post__header, post__body, and post__buttons.

- The post__header contains an avatar icon and another div called post__info, which contains an h2 and p. We show the name and description props here.

- The post__body shows the message prop.

- The post__buttons is calling a component InputOption with Icon, title, and color props. The Icon prop is actually a Material UI icon.

```
import { Avatar } from '@material-ui/core'
import { ChatOutlined, SendOutlined, ShareOutlined, ThumbUpAltOutlined }
from '@material-ui/icons'
import React from 'react'
import InputOption from './InputOption'
import './Post.css'

const Post = ({ name, description, message, photoUrl }) => {
    return (
        <div className="post">
            <div className="post__header">
                <Avatar />
                <div className="post__info">
                    <h2>{name}</h2>
                    <p>{description}</p>
                </div>
            </div>
            <div className="post__body">
                <p>{message}</p>
            </div>
            <div className="post__buttons">
                <InputOption Icon={ThumbUpAltOutlined} title="Like"
                color="gray" />
                <InputOption Icon={ChatOutlined} title="Comment"
                color="gray" />
                <InputOption Icon={ShareOutlined} title="Share"
                color="gray" />
```

```
                <InputOption Icon={SendOutlined} title="Send" color="gray" />
            </div>
        </div>
    )
}

export default Post
```

Now, we will style this component in a `Post.css` file.

```css
.post{
    background-color: white;
    padding: 15px;
    margin-bottom: 10px;
    border-radius: 10px;
}

.post__header{
    display:flex;
    margin-bottom: 10px;
}

.post__info{
    margin-left: 10px;
}

.post__info > p{
    font-size: 12px;
    color: gray;
}

.post__info > h2{
    font-size: 15px;
}

.post__body{
    overflow-wrap: anywhere;
}
```

```
.post__buttons{
    display: flex;
    justify-content: space-evenly;
}
```

Now, on localhost, we will see a nice posting section, as shown in Figure 5-9.

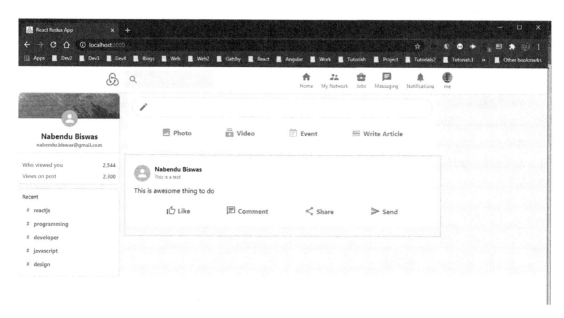

Figure 5-9. *Post example*

Integrating Firebase with React

We will be now integrating Firebase into our project. The first thing to do is install Firebase in our project by running the following command from the terminal.

```
npm install firebase
```

Next, you will update our `firebase.js` file to use the config to initialize the app. After that, use Firestore as the database. We are also using authentication in the project.

```
import firebase from 'firebase'

const firebaseConfig = {
    ...
    ...
};
```

```
const firebaseApp = firebase.initializeApp(firebaseConfig)
const db = firebaseApp.firestore()
const auth = firebase.auth()

export { auth, db }
```

Now, back in Feed.js, we are first importing the required things. After that, we will create two state variables: posts and input.

Now, inside useEffect, we will call Firebase to get the posts collection and then take the snapshot. In Firebase terms, it is the live data, which we will get instantly. We will then set this data in the posts array, via setPosts().

We also have a sendPost(), which will be linked to onClick soon. Here, we are adding a post to Firebase. The message will be taken from the input field, and timestamp is the server timestamp. We are hard-coding the rest of the fields.

Now, inside the return statement in the Feed.js file, we are adding value and onChange to the input field and onClick to the button.

After that, we are mapping through the posts array and passing different props from Firebase to the Post component. The updated code for this is shown in bold here:

```
import React, { useEffect, useState } from 'react'
import { db } from '../firebase'
import firebase from 'firebase'

const Feed = () => {
    const [posts, setPosts] = useState([])
    const [input, setInput] = useState('')

    useEffect(() => {
    db.collection('posts').orderBy('timestamp', 'desc').
    onSnapshot(snapshot => {
    setPosts(snapshot.docs.map(doc => ({
    id: doc.id,
    data: doc.data()
    })))
    })
    }, [])
```

```
const sendPost = e => {
e.preventDefault()
db.collection('posts').add({
name: 'Nabendu Biswas',
description: 'This is a test',
message: input,
photoUrl: '',
timestamp: firebase.firestore.FieldValue.serverTimestamp()
})
setInput('')
}

return (
<div className="feed">
<div className="feed__inputContainer">
<div className="feed__input">
    <Create />
    <form>
    <input value={input} onChange={e => setInput(e.target.value)}
    type="text" />
    <button onClick={sendPost} type="submit">Send
    </button>
    </form>
</div>
<div className="feed__inputOptions">
            ...
</div>
</div>
{posts.map(({ id, data }) => (
<Post
    key={id}
    name={data.name}
    description={data.description}
    message={data.message}
    photoUrl={data.photoUrl}
/>
```

```
    ))}
    </div>
    )
}
```

export default Feed

Now, whenever we type something in the input box and press Enter, it is shown in
real time in our app, as shown in Figure 5-10.

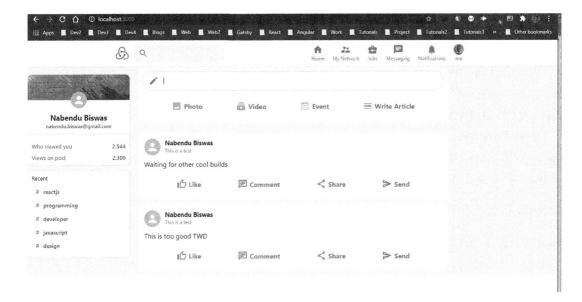

Figure 5-10. *Real time*

Integrating Redux

We will now be integrating Redux into our project. Redux will be used to take the user
details and store them in the global state so that they are available in all components.

Because we have already added Redux to the project while creating it, we need to
remove some boilerplate code. Inside the features\counter folder, delete the Counter.
js and Counter.module.css files.

Next, move the counterSlice.js file to the features folder and delete the empty
counter folder.

Now, in the `store.js` file, change the name, as we want a user and not a counter. Also, change the `counterSlice.js` filename to `userSlice.js`. The updated code for this is shown in bold here:

```
import { configureStore } from '@reduxjs/toolkit';
import userReducer from '../features/userSlice';

export const store = configureStore({
  reducer: {
    user: userReducer,
  },
});
```

Now, update `userSlice.js` with the following content. Here, we have the initial state of the user. After that, we have `login` and `logout` inside the reducers. Both of them change the user state.

We are exporting the `login` and `logout`, which we will use soon to change the state. We are also exporting `selectUser`, through which we can get the user state at any point in time. The code for this is shown here:

```
import { createSlice } from '@reduxjs/toolkit';

export const userSlice = createSlice({
  name: 'user',
  initialState: {
    user: null,
  },
  reducers: {
    login: (state, action) => {
      state.user =  action.payload;
    },
    logout: state => {
      state.user = null;
    },
  },
});

export const { login, logout } = userSlice.actions;
```

```
export const selectUser = state => state.user.user;

export default userSlice.reducer;
```

Now, when we go to localhost and open the Redux devtool, we can see our global Redux state of the user, as shown in Figure 5-11.

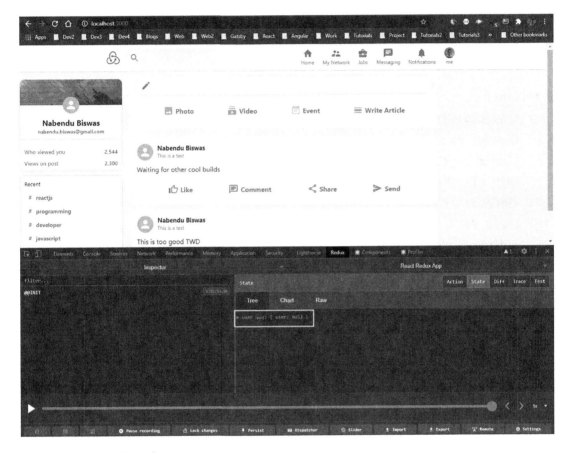

Figure 5-11. *Global state*

Building the Login Page

In this section, we will build our login page and use Redux. So, create two files called Login.js and Login.css in the components folder.

Make the following changes in the App.js file. Here, we are first importing the useSelector and selectUser and then the Login component.

Also, we are using the useSelector hook from react-redux. Inside the return element, if the user is not available, we are showing the Login component or else the other components. The updated code is shown in bold here:

```
import { useSelector } from 'react-redux';
import { selectUser } from './features/userSlice';
import Login from './components/Login';

function App() {
  const user = useSelector(selectUser)

  return (
    <div className="app">
    <Header />
    {!user ? (<Login />) : (
    <div className="app__body">
    <Sidebar />
    <Feed />
    </div>
    )}
    </div>
  );
}

export default App;
```

Now, in the Login.js file, put the following content. Here, we are showing an image and then a form containing four input fields and one button.

We also have a paragraph outside the form, which contains a span to register.

```
import React from 'react'
import './Login.css'

const Login = () => {
    const register = () => {}
    const loginToApp = () => {}

return (
        <div className="login">
            <img src="logo512.png" alt="logo"/>
```

```
        <form>
            <input type="text" placeholder="Full name (required if
            registering)" />
            <input type="text" placeholder="Profile pic URL
            (optional)" />
            <input type="email" placeholder="Email" />
            <input type="password" placeholder="Password" />
            <button type="submit" onClick={loginToApp}>Sign In
            </button>
        </form>
        <p>Not a member?{' '}
            <span onClick={register} className="login__
            register">Register Now</span>
        </p>
    </div>
  )
}

export default Login
```

Also, add the following styles in the Login.css file:

```
.login{
    display: grid;
    place-items: center;
    margin-left: auto;
    margin-right: auto;
    padding-top: 100px;
    padding-bottom: 100px;
}

.login > img{
    object-fit: contain;
    height: 70px;
    margin-top: 20px;
    margin-bottom: 20px;
}
```

```
.login > form{
    display: flex;
    flex-direction: column;
}

.login > form > input{
    width: 350px;
    height: 50px;
    font-size: 20px;
    padding-left: 10px;
    margin-bottom: 10px;
    border-radius: 5px;
}

.login > form > button{
    width: 365px;
    height: 50px;
    font-size: large;
    color: #fff;
    background-color: #0074b1;
    border-radius: 5px;
}

.login__register{
    color: #0177b7;
    cursor: pointer;
}

.login > p{
    margin-top: 20px;
}
```

Now, our login screen will look like Figure 5-12 on localhost.

Figure 5-12. *Login screen*

Adding Email Authentication

Now, we will add email authentication to our app, so we have to enable it from the Firebase console first.

So, click the **Authentication** tab and then the **Get started** button, as shown in Figure 5-13.

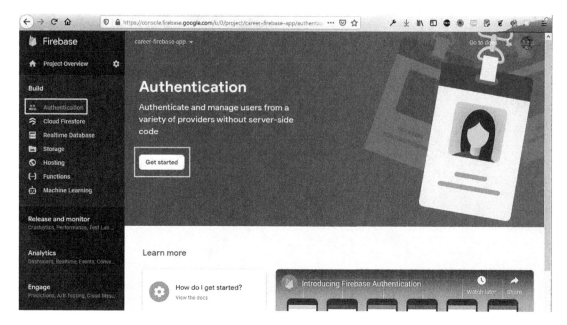

Figure 5-13. *Authentication*

After that, hover over Email/Password and click the edit icon, as shown in Figure 5-14.

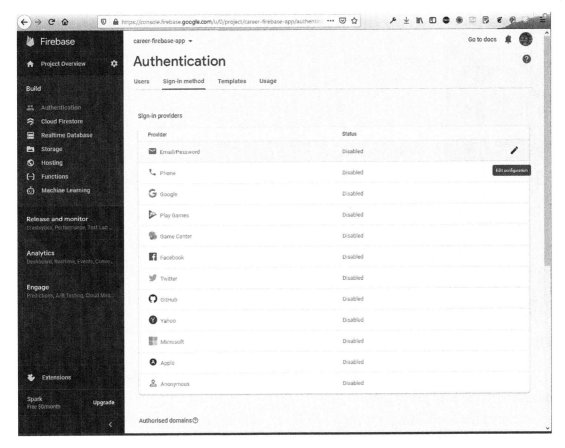

Figure 5-14. *Email configuration*

In the pop-up, click the **Enable** button and then the **Save** button, as shown in Figure 5-15.

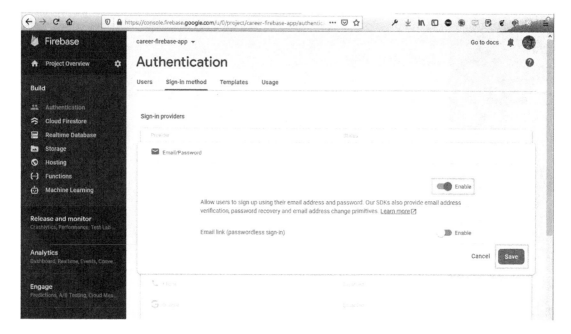

Figure 5-15. *Enable button*

Now, in the `Login.js` file, we will create four different state variables for `email`, `password`, `name`, and `profilePic`.

We are also completing our `register` function here. Inside the function, we will return back, if the user doesn't enter a name. After that, we are using the `createUserWithEmailAndPassword` from Firebase to register the user.

After the registration is done, we are using the `dispatch` function from Redux to send the login to set the global state. The updated code is shown in bold here:

```
import React, { useState }  from 'react'
import { useDispatch } from 'react-redux'
import { auth } from '../firebase'
import { login } from '../features/userSlice'

const Login = () => {
    const [email, setEmail] = useState('')
    const [password, setPassword] = useState('')
    const [name, setName] = useState('')
    const [profilePic, setProfilePic] = useState('')
    const dispatch = useDispatch()
    const register = () => {
```

```
if(!name) return alert('Please enter a Full Name')
auth.createUserWithEmailAndPassword(email,password)
.then(userAuth => userAuth.user.updateProfile({ displayName: name,
photoURL: profilePic })
.then(() => {
dispatch(login({ email: userAuth.user.email, uid: userAuth.user.uid,
displayName: name, photoUrl: profilePic }))
}))
}

    const loginToApp = (e) => {}

return (
    <div className="login">
    <img src="logo512.png" alt="logo"/>
    <form>
    <input value={name} onChange={e => setName(e.target.value)}
    type="text" placeholder="Full name (required if registering)" />
    <input value={profilePic} onChange={e => setProfilePic(e.target.
    value)} type="text" placeholder="Profile pic URL (optional)" />
    <input value={email} onChange={e => setEmail(e.target.value)}
    type="email" placeholder="Email" />
    <input value={password} onChange={e => setPassword(e.target.value)}
    type="password" placeholder="Password" />
    <button type="submit" onClick={loginToApp}>Sign In</button>
    </form>
    ...
    </div>
    )
}

export default Login
```

Now, on localhost when we give the full name, profile picture, email, and password, and click Register Now, we will be taken directly to all components, because in App.js the user will not be blank, as shown in Figure 5-16.

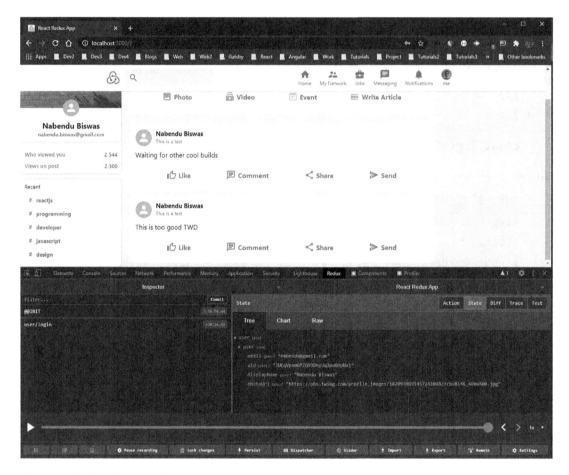

Figure 5-16. *User login*

Now, we want to persist the login because if we refresh, we are taken back to the Register page.

So, in the App.js file, we will use the dispatch and login methods again. But we will check login from within a useEffect, where we are checking it from onAuthStateChanged. The updated code is shown in bold here:

```
import React, { useEffect }  from 'react';
import { useDispatch, useSelector } from 'react-redux';
import { login, selectUser } from './features/userSlice';
import { auth } from './firebase';

function App() {
  const user = useSelector(selectUser)
  const dispatch = useDispatch()

  useEffect(() => {
    auth.onAuthStateChanged(userAuth => {
    if(userAuth){
    dispatch(login({ email: userAuth.email, uid: userAuth.uid,
    displayName: userAuth.displayName, photoUrl: userAuth.
    photoUrl }))
    }
    })
  },[])

  return (
    ...
  );
}

export default App;
```

Now, we will add the functionality to log out when we click the picture in the header. So, in the Header.js file, update the code to the following. Here, we are first importing the required things and after that in props sending the onClick, which runs the logoutApp().

Inside the logoutApp function, we are just dispatch for the logout for Redux and the auth.signout() for Firebase. The updated code is shown in bold here:

```
import { useDispatch } from 'react-redux'
import { logout } from '../features/userSlice'
import { auth } from '../firebase'
```

```
const Header = () => {
    const dispatch = useDispatch()
    const logoutApp = () => {
    dispatch(logout())
    auth.signOut()
    }

    return (
    <div className="header">
            <div className="header__left">

                ...

            </div>
            <div className="header__right">

                ...

            <HeaderOption avatar="https://pbs.twimg.com/profile_
            images/1020939891457241088/fcbu814K_400x400.jpg" title="me"
            onClick={logoutApp} />
            </div>
        </div>

    )
}

export default Header
```

Now, we have to update the HeaderOption.js file, from where we will pass onClick as a callback function. The updated code is shown in bold here:

```
const HeaderOption = ({ avatar, Icon, title, onClick }) => {
    return (
    <div onClick={onClick} className="headerOption">

        ...

    </div>
    )
}

export default HeaderOption
```

Now, one thing that is remaining is for the user to log in after registering. For that, in the Login.js file, update loginToApp(). Inside the function, we are using signInWithEmailAndPassword from Firebase to send the email and password, and after that we are dispatching it in Redux.

Now, we can go to localhost and give the email and password and click the **Sign In** button. The updated code is shown in bold here:

```
const Login = () => {
    ...

    const loginToApp = (e) => {
    e.preventDefault()
    auth.signInWithEmailAndPassword(email,password)
    .then((userAuth) => {
        dispatch(login({
        email: userAuth.user.email,
        uid: userAuth.user.uid,
        displayName: userAuth.user.displayName,
        photoUrl: userAuth.user.photoUrl
        }))
    })
    }

    return (
    ...
    )
}

export default Login
```

Using User Information

Now that we have gotten the user information, we will use it in different parts of the application.

We will first change the information in the Sidebar.js file. To use the user data, we need to call useSelector with selectUser. Inside the return statement, we are using it in Avatar, username, and email. The updated code is shown in bold here:

```
import { useSelector } from 'react-redux'
import { selectUser } from '../features/userSlice'

const Sidebar = () => {
    const user = useSelector(selectUser)

  ...

    return (
    <div className="sidebar">
        <div className="sidebar__top">
        <img src="background.jpg" alt="Background" />
        <Avatar src={user?.photoUrl} className="sidebar__avatar">
        {user.email[0]}</Avatar>
        <h2>{user.displayName}</h2>
        <h4>{user.email}</h4>
        </div>
        ...
    </div>
    )
}

export default Sidebar
```

Now, in Header.js, instead of passing the hard-coded URL, we will pass the avatar prop a Boolean value in the last HeaderOption. The updated code is shown in bold here:

```
const Header = () => {
  ...

    return (
    <div className="header">
        ...
        <div className="header__right">
            ...
```

```
        <HeaderOption avatar={true} title="me" onClick={logoutApp} />
        </div>
    </div>
    )
}
```

Now, in the HeaderOption.js file, we will use uaeSelector again to get access to the user. After that, we are using the first letter of email or photoUrl. The updated code is shown in bold here:

```
import { useSelector } from 'react-redux'
import { selectUser } from '../features/userSlice'

const HeaderOption = ({ avatar, Icon, title, onClick }) => {
    const user = useSelector(selectUser)

    return (
    <div onClick={onClick} className="headerOption">
        {Icon && <Icon className="headerOption__icon" />}
        {avatar && <Avatar className="headerOption__icon" src={user?.
        photoUrl}>{user?.email[0]}</Avatar>}
        <h3 className="headerOption__title">{title}</h3>
    </div>
    )
}

export default HeaderOption
```

Next, in the Feed.js file, we will use the uaeSelector again to get access to the user. Then we are using it while adding the post. The updated code is shown in bold here:

```
import { useSelector } from 'react-redux'
import { selectUser } from '../features/userSlice'

const Feed = () => {
    const user = useSelector(selectUser)
    ...
```

```
    const sendPost = e => {
    e.preventDefault()
    db.collection('posts').add({
        name: user.displayName,
        description: user.email,
        message: input,
        photoUrl: user.photoUrl || '',
        timestamp: firebase.firestore.FieldValue.serverTimestamp()
    })
    setInput('')
    }

    return (
    ...
    )
}

export default Feed
```

Now, in `Post.js`, we are using the `photoUrl` passed from the `Feed` component. The updated code is shown in bold here:

```
const Post = ({ name, description, message, photoUrl }) => {
return (
        <div className="post">
        <div className="post__header">
        <Avatar src={photoUrl}>{name[0]}</Avatar>
        <div className="post__info">
            <h2>{name}</h2>
            <p>{description}</p>
        <div>
        </div>
        </div>
)
}

export default Post
```

Now, a small fix is needed in `App.css` for our app to look good. The updated code is shown in bold here:

```
.app__body{
  display: flex;
  margin-top: 35px;
  max-width: 1200px;
  margin-left: 20px;
  margin-right: 20px;
}
```

Our app is almost complete and looking good with the user data (Figure 5-17).

Figure 5-17. *Almost complete*

Building the Widget Section

We are going to build our last section, which is the widget section. Create two files, `Widgets.js` and `Widgets.css`, inside the `components` folder. Also, include Widgets component in the `App.js` file. The updated code is shown in bold here:

```
import Widgets from './components/Widgets';

function App() {
    ...
    ...

  return (
      <div className="app">
      <Header />
      {!user ? (<Login />) : (
      <div className="app__body">
      <Sidebar />
      <Feed />
      <Widgets />
      </div>
      )}
      </div>
  );
}

export default App;
```

Now, we will put the following content in the `Widgets.js` file. It is just a static file, where we have a heading and an info icon. After that, we are calling the function `newsArticle`, with different props.

```
import { FiberManualRecord, Info } from '@material-ui/icons'
import React from 'react'
import './Widgets.css'

const Widgets = () => {
    const newsArticle = (heading, subtitle) => (
```

```
        <div className="widgets__article">
            <div className="widgets__articleleft">
                <FiberManualRecord />
            </div>
            <div className="widgets__articleright">
                <h4>{heading}</h4>
                <p>{subtitle}</p>
            </div>
        </div>
    )

return (
    <div className="widgets">
      <div className="widgets__header">
        <h2>Tech News</h2>
        <Info />
      </div>
        {newsArticle("TWD at top with 500k subscriber", "Top news - 9099
        readers")}
        {newsArticle("Qualcomm Snapdragon 775 Series", "Top news - 8760
        readers")}
        {newsArticle("Amazfit T-Rex Pro Hands", "Top news - 999 readers")}
        {newsArticle("Apple Music Service Feature for iOS", "Top news - 899
        readers")}
        {newsArticle("Mars Rover Perseverance Takes First Drive", "Top
        news - 799 readers")}
        {newsArticle("Twitter CEO Jack Dorsey Auctions Tweet", "Top news -
        599 readers")}
    </div>
  )
}

export default Widgets
```

Now, we will put the styles for this in the `Widgets.css` file.

```css
.widgets{
    position: sticky;
    top: 80px;
    flex: 0.2;
    background-color: white;
    border-radius: 10px;
    border: 1px solid lightgray;
    height: fit-content;
    padding-bottom: 10px;
}

.widgets__header{
    display: flex;
    align-items: center;
    justify-content: space-between;
    padding: 10px;
}

.widgets__header > h2{
    font-size: 16px;
    font-weight: 400;
}

.widgets__article{
    display: flex;
    padding: 10px;
    cursor: pointer;
}

.widgets__article:hover{
    background-color: whitesmoke;
}

.widgets__articleleft{
    color: #0177b7;
    margin-left: 5px;
}
```

```css
.widgets__articleleft > .MuiSvgIcon-root{
    font-size: 15px;
}

.widgets__articleright{
    flex: 1;
}

.widgets__articleright > h4{
    font-size: 14px;
}

.widgets__articleright > p{
    font-size: 12px;
    color: gray;
}
```

Our app is complete now! It looks like Figure 5-18.

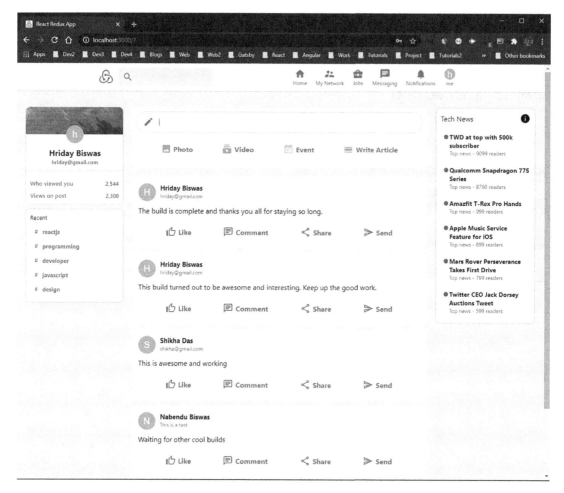

Figure 5-18. *Our final app*

Deploying and Hosting Through Firebase

We can deploy our app in Firebase, and we will follow the same steps as in earlier chapters.

The deployment was successful and works properly (Figure 5-19).

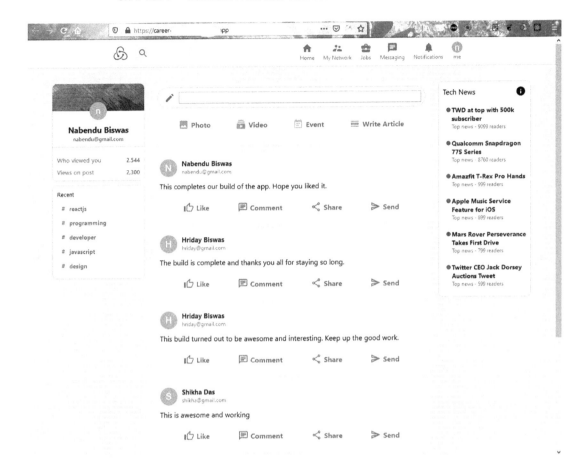

Figure 5-19. *Deployed*

Summary

In this chapter, you learned how to make a career-related social media app, which you can log into through email. You saw how to create the web app with React and also learned to use Redux. You also learned how to do the hosting in Firebase.

Index

A, B

Back-end-as-a-service (BaaS), 1

C, D, E

Career-related social media
app, 129, 130
create-react-app, 130
deployment/hosting, 178, 179
email authentication
App.js, 166, 167
configuration, 162, 163
enable button, 163, 164
getting started, 161, 162
Header.js, 167, 168
HeaderOption.js, 168
Login.js, 164, 165
loginToApp(), 169
logoutApp function, 167
register function, 164
user login, 166
feed component
App.js, 145
divs, 145
Feed.css, 146, 147
InputOption.css, 148
InputOption.js, 147
localhost, 148, 149
firebase setup, 130, 132
header
App.js, 134
divs, 135
Header.css, 136

HeaderOption.css, 137, 138
HeaderOption.js, 137
localhost, 138
npm install, 134
integration
Feed.js, 153
firebase.js, 152
mapping, 153–155
real time, 155
sendPost(), 153
useEffect, 153
login page
App.js, 157, 158
Login.css, 159, 160
Login.js, 158, 159
login screen, 160, 161
useSelector, 158
Post section
divs, 150, 151
Feed.js, 149
localhost, 152
Post.css, 151, 152
React setup, 132, 134
Redux, 155–157
sidebar
add styles, 139
App.js, 138
divs, 139, 140
localhost, 142, 144
recentItem function, 143
Sidebar.css, 140–144
user information, 170–173
widget section, 174–178

© Nabendu Biswas 2022
N. Biswas, *Beginning React and Firebase*, https://doi.org/10.1007/978-1-4842-7812-3

T, U, V, W, X, Y, Z

Printed in the United States
by Baker & Taylor Publisher Services